CRANKING
UP
RUSH

**Concise, fun, high-energy tours through
the catalogs of major musical acts, in just 11 songs**

Series Editor: Arthur Lizie

Other titles in Backbeat's GOES TO 11 series:

CRANKING UP RUSH

THEIR MUSICAL LEGACY IN 11 SONGS

ADRIEN BEGRAND

Backbeat
Books

Backbeat
Books

Bloomsbury Publishing Group, Inc.
Backbeatbooks.com

Distributed by NATIONAL BOOK NETWORK

British Library Cataloguing in Publication Information available

Library of Congress Cataloging-in-Publication Data

Names: Begrand, Adrien, author.
Title: Cranking up Rush: their musical legacy in 11 songs / Adrien Begrand.
Description: Essex, Connecticut: Backbeat, 2024. | Series: Goes to 11 | Includes
    bibliographical references and index.
Identifiers: LCCN 2024023525 | ISBN 9781493084746 (pbk) | ISBN
    9781493084753 (ebook)
Subjects: LCSH: Rush (Musical group) | Progressive rock music—History and
    criticism.
Classification: LCC ML421.R87 B45 2024 | DDC 782.42166092/2dc23/
    eng/20240522
LC record available at https://lccn.loc.gov/2024023525

∞™ The paper used in this publication meets the minimum requirements of
American National Standard for Information Sciences—Permanence of Paper for
Printed Library Materials, ANSI/NISO Z39.48-1992

CONTENTS

INTRODUCTION

Teenage friends debate the themes of "2112" as one of them sifts seeds from marijuana buds using the album's gatefold sleeve. A drum student tries to nail down "Tom Sawyer," dumbstruck by how such a seemingly simple song can be so damned hard to play. A thirteen-year-old outcast hears "Subdivisions" and thinks, finally, someone out there understands them. An office employee sees a coworker with a Rush coffee mug ("You like Rush, too?"), and they become instant friends. An ecstatic crowd in Brazil sings along to "YYZ," even though it's an instrumental. Neil Peart starts his drum solo at a concert in 2015, and a proud dad hoists his young daughter on his shoulders so she can see the master at work. A twelve-year-old buys a cheap used vinyl copy of *Moving Pictures* at a record fair out of curiosity and a day later is obsessed with those three serious-looking guys on the back cover.

Many bands from the 1970s progressive rock era have maintained long, fruitful careers, but none were able to do so as gracefully as Rush did. And none of Rush's prog peers had such a devoted—and nerdily obsessive—fan base. For forty years the Canadian trio of Geddy Lee, Alex Lifeson, and Neil Peart relentlessly pursued musical growth, embracing new ideas with gusto, always thinking ahead, moving with the times. They endured internal strife, personal tragedy, creative peaks and valleys, all while remaining best friends. They did it with an uncompromising attitude, their integrity fully intact, and best of all, with a sense of humor that endeared them to their audience even more. So loved by fans and peers are Rush that when the news broke in January 2020 that Peart had died of brain cancer, the outpouring of emotion worldwide, from fans to well-known artists, was immediate and overwhelming.

Despite selling more than forty-two million albums worldwide, the band didn't receive the respect it deserved from the music "establishment" for decades. It wasn't until Generation X—those of us born between the years 1961 and 1981—reached middle age and started to supplant baby boomer journalists that the mainstream media would change the way they would portray Rush. Suddenly the accolades started pouring in, from their 2013 Rock and Roll Hall of Fame induction to their first *Rolling Stone* cover in 2015. Only in recent years have books about Rush started to surface, like the one you're holding now.

This book will take a different approach than the rest, focusing on eleven of Rush's greatest songs in an effort to explain why this band is so special. Knowing that Rush's discography is so varied that it's impossible to compile a definitive, ranked list of their greatest songs (this is a band that wrote both "What You're Doing" and "Mystic Rhythms"), I've decided to take a different approach. Rush's career trajectory is such a beautiful, bittersweetly perfect arc that the focal point of each chapter will be one song from eleven specific periods in the band's history, from their first album in 1974 to their final studio opus in 2012, with enough context added along the way, as well as a bonus playlist to help round out the story. Besides, there are so many great Rush songs that there's no way anyone could mess up a list of the eleven best ones. There are no wrong answers! Well, unless the list includes "Virtuality"; then we'll have to have a chat.

When it comes to Rush, a lot of people's favorite songs or albums tend to be the first song or album they heard. For me, that's *Grace Under Pressure*, which I heard soon after its release in 1984 when I was thirteen. "Distant Early Warning" had me intrigued, and soon "Red Sector A" had me riveted. I grew up a long way from cities where Rush played, so I devoured any concert footage I could find on TV or VHS tape. When their *Grace Under Pressure* concert aired on Canadian TV in early 1985, it was my first glimpse of the high-tech spectacle that was a Rush show. Soon I was borrowing old '70s Rush albums from my local library and obsessively making tapes, gradually exploring their many mind-bending songs. In my mid-twenties I drifted away from Rush a little, partially preoccupied with present-day indie rock and partially because I couldn't stand *Test for Echo* (sorry, guys), but when the magic returned in 2002 with *Vapor Trails*, I was fully back onboard, this time as a freelance music journalist. Those final thirteen years were a glorious late-career renaissance for Rush, and it was a joy to cover that era, seeing them make strong, vital music, not to mention pulling off one imaginative, innovative stage show after another, right to their final tour in 2015.

Due to copyright restrictions on reprinting actual lyrics from the songs, I advise accessing the lyrics to each song before reading each chapter, so they can give you a frame of reference for the book's narrative. After all, and if you don't know already, Rush's lyrics offer a lot more insight and imagination than much of what you'll find on the heavy metal and hard rock landscape, and you'll witness the personal and philosophical growth of that master lyricist, Neil Peart. Thankfully, Rush's lyrics have been beautifully curated at https://www.rush.com/albums. So, if you want to truly do a deep dive, be sure to keep a browser tab, as well as your mobile audio streamer of choice, open on your device. Turn on, tune in, and venture far through space, time, and back again.

If you're a longtime fan of Rush's music, hopefully this book will provide some fun new perspectives, or at the very least, compel you to track me down and suggest your own list of eleven songs. Which I embrace! If you're new to Rush, welcome to the world's biggest, nerdiest family of misfits and weirdos. You're in for a very fun, rewarding adventure. It's up to you to choose where to start. There's no wrong answer.

1

"WORKING MAN"

Three Travelers of Willowdale

At first glimpse, the name Willowdale sounds like a quaint conjuration from J. R. R. Tolkien's imagination, as though it were a little village in the gently rolling green hills of the Shire, just down the road from Hobbiton, somewhere along the gently winding Brandywine River. At least, that's the impression one gets upon listening to "The Necromancer," a track from Rush's third album, 1975's *Caress of Steel*, whose intro features a narration that mentions three travelers from that seemingly quaint, idyllic locale.

Far from it. Willowdale, Ontario, is one of many suburbs on the northern periphery of Toronto's gigantic urban sprawl, where during the postwar boom of the early 1950s, middle-class Canadians, many of them immigrants, settled to raise their young families. But it's here, in this culturally diverse neighborhood (Italian, Greek, Jewish, Chinese, Slavic, among many others), where the foundation for the most influential Canadian rock band of all time would be laid.

Born on July 29, 1953, Gershon "Gary" Eliezer Weinrib was the son of Moshe "Morris" Weinrib and Manya "Mary" Rubinstein, two Polish Jewish survivors of the Holocaust who met as teens in the Starachowice ghetto and survived imprisonments at Auschwitz, Dachau, and Bergen-Belsen concentration camps during World War II. After the war, Morris—a musician who used to serenade his future wife under her window with his mandolin—and Mary wed and immigrated to Canada, where they opened a variety store in suburban Toronto and raised Gary and his two younger siblings. Sadly, Morris would die in October 1964, leaving eleven-year-old Gary as "the man of the house," a title unfairly foisted upon him by his extended family.

Like his father, Gary showed an acumen for music, first taking piano lessons at the age of nine. Like millions of other kids in 1964, Gary was a huge fan of the Beatles and obsessively listened to rock 'n' roll on the radio. Although by the end of 1964 Gary would own his first guitar, music would have to take a back seat as he would be required to complete his Yud Bet Chodesh as per his Jewish faith: twelve months of mourning, during which listening to music is forbidden. To a young rock 'n' roll–obsessed boy in 1964 that's an eternity, a devastating blow, but Gary, true to his faith and loyal to his mother, honored the tradition as he prepared to enter junior high school.

Aleksandar Živojinović was born on August 27, 1953, in the mountain town of Fernie, British Columbia, to parents Nenad and Melanija, two Serbian immigrants from Yugoslavia. Nenad worked in a nearby mine but suffered a back injury when Alex was two years old, and shortly after, in April 1955, the family moved to suburban Toronto. Melanija, who was all too familiar with racial turmoil in Yugoslavia, encouraged Alex and his sister to respect racial diversity, and the effervescent Alex thrived in culturally rich Willowdale, his humorous antics endearing him to his classmates.

Like Gary Weinrib's parents, Nenad and Melanija encouraged Alex to pursue a musical education, and as a preteen he started taking viola lessons. A kid in the early 1960s, with the youth culture exploding around him, Alex was gifted an eleven-dollar Kent classical guitar for Christmas in 1965. Hungry for an amplifier, Alex saved up for a cheap Kent amp but taped the word "Vox" to it to make it look more professional. Eventually, the now-obsessed young musician bought a fifty-nine-dollar Conora solid-body electric guitar, which he would paint in psychedelic colors, just like his hero, Eric Clapton of Cream.

At Fisherville Junior High, Gary—whose nickname had become "Geddy" after the way his mother would pronounce his name in her Yiddish accent—had a buddy named Steve Shutt, who happened to know a goofy kid named Alex Živojinović. Geddy was pretty good at guitar, as was Alex, and Steve suggested the two of them get together and jam sometime. Geddy and Alex quickly hit it off, bonding over their desire to learn their favorite British Invasion songs. Geddy would decide to take up the bass, and the jam sessions began in earnest. As for their mutual friend Steve, he preferred hockey, and would go on to have a Hall of Fame career as a star forward for the Montreal Canadiens in the 1970s. But that's another story.

New best friends Geddy and Alex would jam loudly for hours at a time in the basement of Geddy's house. At that time, it was all mere fun for the two thirteen-year-olds, and things didn't start to get serious until Alex's friend John Rutsey came along. Although he was only months older than Alex and Geddy, John was a lot more mature, outgoing, and forward-thinking, not to mention a damn good drummer and a more stylish dresser than the other two. Geddy and Alex would eventually grow into a phenomenal collaborative team, but it wouldn't have happened without the influence of the ambitious Rutsey in those early days.

As close as they were, Geddy and Alex would not perform in a proper, working rock band together until 1968, when they had just turned fifteen. Remarkably experienced for a young teenager, Rutsey would play in local bands the Guilde and Summer Wind before forming the Lost Cause with Alex in late 1967. That band would split, and Alex and John would form the Projection the following year. Neither were big fans of that band name, and John's brother Bill suggested a shorter name, something that would feel immediate, impactful. One name he came up with was Rush, which John took an instant liking to.

With bassist Jeff Jones, Rush played their first gig at the Coff-In, located in the basement of St. Theodore of Canterbury Anglican Church, on September 18, 1968. Jones, who viewed Rush as a casual project, was a no-show for Rush's second show a week later, and Alex called Geddy to fill in on bass and vocals. After a hasty two-hour rehearsal, the first classic incarnation of Rush played its inaugural gig, which went so well that the trio started booking all-ages shows across Toronto. Because they were all underage (the legal drinking age in Ontario was twenty-one at the time) Rutsey, Weinrib, and Živojinović cleverly booked high school dances, playing in school gymnasiums on weekends. By connecting face-to-face with teenagers, rock 'n' roll's most important demographic, Rush steadily made a name for themselves on the local circuit.

In 1969, aspiring promoter Ray Danniels showed interest in the band and soon became their manager. Personalities initially clashed between Danniels and Weinrib, and Geddy was ousted from the band. Rutsey and Živojinović would form Hadrian, while Weinrib would form a couple of heavy blues rock bands called Ogilvie and Judd. At the same time, a band called Led Zeppelin released their epochal debut album, which had a transformative influence on seventeen-year old Weinrib.

Zeppelin's mastery of heavy blues dynamics—on full display on such songs as "What Is and What Shall Never Be" and "How Many More Times"—permanently changed how far a rock 'n' roll band could go: John Bonham's drums sounded massive, Jimmy Page's riffs were towering, John Paul Jones anchored those monstrous grooves with grace and power, and Robert Plant could scream like no rock singer had screamed before. Or at least since Little Richard. As soon as he heard Plant howling away, Weinrib followed suit and began singing in his soon-to-be trademark upper-register scream.

By September of 1969 Hadrian had imploded, leaving John and Alex without a band. With Judd petering out as well, the timing was perfect: Danniels contacted Weinrib, fences were mended, and Rush was back intact. Permanently.

By 1971 Rush were starting to gain serious momentum. John, Geddy, and Alex bonded over the heavier guitar bands at the time— Cream, Led Zeppelin, Blue Cheer, Jimi Hendrix—and their sound started to reflect it. The boys would cover songs by those artists, as well as tracks by the Yardbirds, Jeff Beck, John Mayall, Ten Years After, and Traffic. The more experience they acquired, the more confident Geddy and Alex felt when it came to composition, and the high school sets started to feature original music. Still, though, it was left to the gregarious Rutsey to banter with audiences and introduce songs from behind his kit because his bandmates were too shy.

When Ontario dropped the legal drinking age from twenty-one to eighteen on January 1, 1971, it was perfect timing for Rush. On the cusp of turning eighteen themselves, Rutsey, Živojinović, and Weinrib had honed their skills over the past year and were fully prepared to play the local bar circuit. Rush would play their first club show that spring and would gradually play more and more shows in Toronto through 1972, even touring northern Ontario, playing to rough crowds in gritty small-town bars. Meanwhile, Geddy and Alex decided to take on stage names: Gary Weinrib chose to combine his long-running nickname and his middle name. Alex Živojinović, on the other hand, had a clever idea. Translated semi-literally from Serbian, "Živojinović" means "son of life" in English, so Alex decided to have some fun with it. From then on, it would be Geddy Lee and Alex Lifeson, an inseparable duo that would eventually become known the world over.

In 1973 the three twenty-year-olds were already veterans of the Toronto music scene, on the verge of outgrowing it in fact, and the next logical step was a debut album. Sadly, for Ray Danniels and Rush, there were no takers. The Canadian mainstream music scene circa 1973 could be generously described as idiosyncratic. The homegrown music that was charting at the time was either soft rock, folk, pure schmaltz, or all of the above: Anne Murray, Terry Jacks, Gordon Lightfoot, Ian Thomas, the Stampeders. April Wine was still years away from embracing riff rock, and the Guess Who always held the volume of their otherwise fun music back a degree or two. By comparison, Rush sounded far too aggressive for the Canadian mainstream, and considering Geddy Lee's piercing wail, too extreme. The only mainstream Canadian band that came closest to Rush's boisterousness was Bachman-Turner Overdrive, who within a year would be blowing up all over the United States, which in time would help Rush immeasurably. But we'll get to that part.

Although heavy rock was just starting to percolate in America (Montrose's landmark debut album came out in 1973, as did Blue Öyster Cult's *Tyranny and Mutation*), the bulk of that style of music was still coming out of the UK: Deep Purple, Led Zeppelin, Black Sabbath, Budgie, King Crimson, Status Quo, Foghat, Hawkwind, Wishbone Ash, Uriah Heep, Nazareth. The US record labels' attitude toward new artists was to wait and see what the next trend would be, and even worse, the Canadian attitude was to wait and see which Canadian band attracted attention from the Americans. Ray Danniels had no other choice than to create his own independent label, Moon Records, and in spring 1973 Rush booked some cheap, after-midnight time in Eastern Sound Studios with producer Dave Stock to lay down tracks that would hopefully become that first long player.

For their first single, Rush released a cover of the Buddy Holly standard "Not Fade Away," an audience favorite at Rush's bar shows. Backing "Not Fade Away" on the B-side was the Rush original "You Can't Fight It," written by Lee and Rutsey in 1971. Its lively boogie is decent, but it pales in comparison to what folks would hear from the band a year later. Stock, whose background was English pop, didn't exactly know how to get the best out of such a riff-driven band as Rush, and the resulting single sounded watered-down to the point of flavorless. While the single sold out—Manya Weinrib's store in Newmarket bought plenty of copies—the band was frustrated with the results of their first time in the studio.

Enter Terry Brown. Like Stock, Brown was a British expat residing in Toronto, but he had a much deeper rock background than his peer. As a young mixer and recording engineer in London, he worked with Jimi Hendrix, Joe Cocker, Traffic, Procol Harum, and, most notably, the Who. Brown knew how to record a heavy, guitar-based band. His experience working with the Who's John Entwistle was especially valuable to Geddy Lee, who cited "The

Ox" as a major influence on his style of bass playing. Additionally, Brown was familiar with mainstream tastes in production, having worked on the first three April Wine albums as well as the Stampeders' skiffle-esque smash 1971 single "Sweet City Woman." Here was a guy who knew how to make a rock trio sound palatable on record without compromising their sound. This pairing of producer and band would turn into a phenomenal partnership for nearly the next decade, but those first steps were taken in November 1973 as Brown and the boys commenced work at Toronto Sound Studios.

Released in Canada on Moon Records on March 1, 1974, the eponymous *Rush* was exactly what the band strove to put out: a gritty collection of eight hard-driving songs in the vein of their heroes, featuring production that made the music burst out of speakers. The album unapologetically wears its influences on its sleeve, namely Cream and Led Zeppelin, and those obvious signposts would follow the band throughout 1974, as many music critics, while praising the band's energy, often dismissed the music as lacking originality.

Without question, it's easy to hear those similarities throughout the record. Opening track "Finding My Way" is the one song on *Rush* that feels the most Zeppelin-esque: Lifeson's nimble-fingered opening riff fades in, growing louder and louder, until Rutsey's cymbals crash loudly and Lee announces his presence with a flamboyant, high-pitched scream à la Robert Plant. He might be shouting about finding his way to a girl, but over five decades later it feels more like a mission statement: they have a lot of living and growing to do, and they're determined to somehow find their way in their art, their career, and their life. With its well-timed tempo changes and attention-grabbing stops and starts, it's a riveting opening salvo.

The concise "Need Some Love" and the Southern-fried "Take a Friend" keep the mood light, as does Lee's oddly charming "In the Mood." The latter song somehow rises above Geddy's lyrics ("Well-a hey now, bay-beh") and turns into a snappy little rocker that, while not exactly searing, still has some grit. On the other hand, two deep cuts serve as glimpses of what Rush would be capable of within the year. The wistful "Before and After" contains subtle echoes of Yes in its sunny opening instrumental section, while the wonderfully dynamic seven-and-a-half-minute "Here Again" shows how powerful a tool restraint can be for a heavy rock band, and it's executed well by Rush.

Rush might be a good debut album, but its great moments are when Lee, Lifeson, and Rutsey lock themselves into a caveman groove and hammer out some glorious, knuckle-dragging jams. "What You're Doing" cockily struts like Led Zeppelin's "Heartbreaker," and the riff is so damned contagious that Lee's lyrics almost feel like an afterthought. It's all about that groove, best epitomized on the album's final track, which thanks to some good timing and luck would get Rush their coveted record deal.

If you're going to write a song called "Working Man," it had better be simple, straight to the point, devoid of subtlety. To this day, music for the blue-collar crowd still leans heavily toward guitar-based artists, and if an artist is going to sing from the perspective of a lowly shift worker, they had better get it right. You don't even have to have blue-collar experience—Bruce Springsteen will be the first to tell you that he was never a real "working man"—but the key thing is that you have to sell it. You have to sound absolutely convincing, because fans of that music can spot a phony the moment they hear it.

Perhaps it's because Geddy Lee and Alex Lifeson came from families that valued hard work and discipline, or perhaps it's because since dropping out of twelfth grade they worked like dogs to even get a chance at playing music for people. Either way, they were driven and deeply passionate, and whether the callouses on your fingers are from construction or from playing electric guitar, what matters most is that the music feels genuine. And "Working Man" is as simple and as genuine as it gets.

Rush announce their presence with authority on the opening notes of "Working Man." Again, it's an extremely simple progression, just like "Smoke on the Water" or "Iron Man," four notes on the fifth and sixth strings that even the rawest newbie could learn in minutes: E, D, A . . . E, C, D. It sounds quaint when you're practicing it, but amplified thousands of watts it becomes a towering, gargantuan riff that stands alongside the gods Page, Iommi, and Blackmore. It's interesting how a record so indebted to the swagger of Cream and Led Zeppelin would be upstaged by a dark, ominous riff that sounds more like Black Sabbath, and it's smart that the band saved that moment for last. It brings the album to a thrilling climax, starting with Alex's solo riff, and then

Geddy's impassioned first verse dwelling on the drudgery of day-to-day life at a dead-end job.

Rutsey enters with his heavy-hitting beats, punctuating Geddy's lines with thuds and cymbal crashes as the verse continues, the narrator realizing that there might be more to life than being a faceless cog in the machine.

A songwriter choosing to depict the working class could easily be tempted to take a snarkier tone, poking fun at those who find themselves stuck in a lousy job, selling the fantasy of being a traveling rock star who has all the time in the world to do whatever they want. As it so happens, Bachman-Turner Overdrive's single "Takin' Care of Business," a song that does just that, was starting to make big waves in America in early summer 1974. People dug the humor of the song's satirical notion that you could just quit your job, get in with the right kind of fellows, and sit back and work at nothin' all day. It was simple, it was fun, it was stupidly catchy.

"Working Man," however, goes for gravitas instead of humor, which is a big reason why the lyrics, straightforward as they are, hit so hard. The narrator knows he's stuck in a rut, working to live rather than living to work. He gets up early, comes home at five, takes a moment to enjoy a cold beer, and it's back to the grind again. He senses he can find a way out, but he just needs another paycheck first. Just one more, and he'll start saving toward whatever his dream is. Maybe a few paychecks. Or six months. Well, if he's being realistic, a year. That sadness permeates the song; it understands its subject deeply. Life is hard, work can be hard, and you try like mad to find just a little transcendence amid the drudgery.

Similarly, "Working Man" smartly shifts toward something resembling transcendence. After a soulful, melancholy solo by Lifeson, the band stops suddenly at the two-minute mark and immediately shifts gears into a four-on-the-floor groove, Rutsey locked in a tempo that bears an uncanny resemblance to the motorik beat of early-'70s krautrock: head down, locked in 4/4 time with little variation save for a couple fills. This section becomes a fantastic showcase for Lifeson's skills as a stadium rock shredder, and he guides his mates through a fiery little journey, his solo ebbing and flowing, building tension and releasing it. It's a fantastic three-minute song-within-a-song, as though the track's protagonist has found a few moments to briefly escape reality. It's upbeat, optimistic, but reality comes crashing down as it always does, and the song returns to that monumental opening riff. That reverie is now a distant memory, and the sadness of it all is hammered home by Rutsey, whose cymbal crashes and drum fills are his most powerful on the entire album, stabbing like daggers to the heart as the narrator's resignation evokes devastating hopelessness.

In May 1974 Donna Halper, music director at WMMS FM in Cleveland, Ohio, received a promo LP from her friend and colleague Bob Roper at Warner Music Canada. On May 24, she played "Working Man" for the first time. Comically, the phone lines lit up with dozens of listeners asking to know more about this amazing new track by Led Zeppelin, and when the new Zep album was coming out. Requests for "Working Man" soon came pouring in, more Midwest radio stations picked up on the track, and record stores imported as many copies of the Moon Records release as they could.

At the same time, Rush was a week into their first run of shows in the United States, inching their way through the Midwest, and by the time they got to Cleveland, manager Danniels had booked them to open for ZZ Top, which would be their biggest concert to date. The groundswell from word-of-mouth publicity was starting to feel palpable, and American record labels came sniffing. The band almost signed with Casablanca Records, which had recently signed New York City upstarts Kiss, but right before they signed on the dotted line the band got a call from Cliff Burnstein, an A&R rep for Mercury Records in Chicago, who also backed BTO, whose breakthrough single was blowing up across the country. Burnstein had heard the album on a Monday morning and was so blown away by it that after several frantic phone calls—including one to Rush begging them not to sign with Casablanca before he could get an offer to them—a five-year, $200,000 deal, including a $75,000 advance, was set up by the end of the day, and Danniels and Rush signed shortly thereafter.

Little did Mercury know that Rush was in the middle of some internal issues when they signed the band. Rutsey, a type 1 diabetic, was struggling. Suddenly more and more shows were lined up, and John couldn't balance the band, the partying, and his health. A fan of the simpler side of heavy rock, he also wasn't thrilled with the sound of Alex and Geddy's new material, which was starting to become more complex, more influenced by Yes and King Crimson. After signing with Mercury, Lee and Lifeson were ecstatic at the thought of affording new gear, but John was miserable, often disconnecting from his two bandmates, and within the tight-knit confines of a traveling rock band, that's cancerous. Rush were now contractually obligated to continue with a heavy tour itinerary, and if that meant going on without John Rutsey behind the kit, so be it. They'd have to find another drummer.

Chapter One Playlist:

"I Can't Explain," The Who

"Crossroads," Cream

"Stroll On," The Yardbirds

"Beck's Bolero," Jeff Beck

"Summertime Blues," Blue Cheer

"How Many More Times," Led Zeppelin

"Last Song," Edward Bear

"Sweet City Woman," The Stampeders

"Rock the Nation," Montrose

"Caroline," Status Quo

"Takin' Care of Business," Bachman-Turner Overdrive

2

"ANTHEM"

Neil Peart, Parts Manager

On a hot July day in 1974, a brown Ford Pinto pulled up to Rush's rehearsal space on Liverpool Road in Ajax, Ontario. Out stepped a gangly, six-foot-three kid with short hair who proceeded to pull out a couple garbage cans from the little car's hatchback. Compared to Geddy Lee and Alex Lifeson, who were long-haired, flush with cash and new gear, wearing velvet pants and platform shoes, and driving sports cars, this dude from the sticks looked ridiculous.

Vic Wilson at Anthem Entertainment had learned of a talented drummer from St. Catherines, Ontario, via a fellow named Johnny Trojan, himself a drummer for Curtis Lee, another band Anthem managed at the time. Neil Peart had just returned from London, England, where he attempted—unsuccessfully—to make inroads in the UK heavy rock scene, and he was currently working at his father's farm implements dealership to make ends meet. Apparently he was big into Keith Moon and Ginger Baker, he was looking for work, and after being coerced by Rush's management to audition, he decided to give it a shot. Inside those garbage cans stuffed into his mom's Pinto was a drum kit featuring two comically small eighteen-inch kick drums, and when he sat behind the set-up kit, he loomed over it like a giant. Surely this guy can't be serious. As soon as he started playing, though, he hit his drums with astonishing power and precision, his maniacal triplets echoing Cream and the Who at the same time. This guy was very serious indeed.

Neil Ellwood Peart was born on September 12, 1952, in Hamilton, Ontario, the first of four children to Glen and Betty Peart. When Neil was two years old, the young family moved from their farm near Hagersville, Ontario, sixty miles east to St. Catherines. A precociously smart kid, Neil was moved up a grade in elementary school twice, which only perpetuated his disinterest in schooling. Besides, it's no fun for a twelve-year-old to enter ninth grade. The fact was that Neil was an autodidact, perfectly happy to lose himself in books and learn on his own, save for one passion.

Like his future Rush bandmates, Neil grew up in a household that appreciated music. His uncle, who was only a year older than him, played in a local R&B band, and thanks to the little transistor radio his mom gifted him, Neil quickly started obsessing over the Hit Parade's pre-Beatles R&B hits that stations in Toronto and Buffalo, New York, would spin. He would hear such artists as James Brown, Wilson Pickett, and Otis Redding, and would become particularly transfixed by two songs as a teenager: Carole King's shuffling "Chains," recorded by the Cookies in 1962, and Sam & Dave's raw, insistent 1966 classic "Hold On, I'm Comin'."

The real clincher, though, would be seeing Sal Mineo in the 1959 film *The Gene Krupa Story*, and after pestering his parents for a couple years, he would receive a pair of sticks and a practice pad. "If you stick with this pad for a year," they told him, "then we'll talk about drums."

With only two weeks to rehearse for a tour opening for Uriah Heep and Manfred Mann, Peart was quickly hired, and the new trio played their first show together on August 14, 1974, to a crowd of eleven thousand at the Pittsburgh Civic Arena. Over the next four months, Rush would undertake an intense schedule, opening for the likes of Kiss, Blue Öyster Cult, Hawkwind, T. Rex, Nazareth, Foghat, and Rory Gallagher. On the road constantly, with few days off, the tour was a perfect opportunity for Peart, Lee, and Lifeson to get to know one another, and as the camaraderie grew, the threesome began to develop exciting new music, written and arranged between shows.

To put it politely, the lyrics Lee and Lifeson wrote, while serviceable, lacked the imagination the new, increasingly more aggressive and complex material demanded. Peart, whose nose was constantly in a book—much to the bafflement of Kiss—was more articulate than your average heavy rock drummer, so at the behest of his new bandmates, he assumed the role of lyricist. To have a drummer that was equal parts Keith Moon and Bill Bruford was an incredible ingredient for the rapidly developing Rush; for that same drummer to display an acumen for the written word, for fantasy storytelling, was akin to striking gold. Better yet for Peart, being given such a big responsibility so soon after joining the band quickly made him feel included, making it easier to fit in as "the new guy."

Two new songs, "Best I Can" and "In the End," were written before Peart joined the band, but he would write the lyrics for the other six songs that would make up the album *Fly By Night*. Swiftly recorded and mixed with Terry Brown during a five-day December break between performances and released on February 15, 1975, *Fly By Night* was a startling change in direction from the comparatively straightforward debut, with songs that ranged from fiery metal anthems ("Beneath, Between & Behind") to wistful tales of travel ("Fly By Night") to contemplative Tolkien-derived ballads ("Rivendell") to Rush's first foray into the structurally complex songwriting that would define their 1970s work ("By-Tor and the Snow Dog").

By 1974, British progressive rock was dominant. Yes, whom Geddy Lee was a particular fan of, were at their creative and commercial peak thanks to landmark albums *Fragile*, *Close to the Edge*, and *Tales of Topographic Oceans*. Genesis was making serious waves with *Selling England by the Pound* and *The Lamb Lies Down on Broadway*. Emerson, Lake & Palmer's *Brain Salad Surgery* was so popular that the band headlined the massive California Jam in April 1974 in front of a quarter million people, complete with spinning grand piano. King Crimson reinvented themselves as a formidable power trio of their own on the stunning *Red* album. Even the heavier bands were dabbling in prog: Yes's Rick Wakeman played on Black Sabbath's *Sabbath Bloody Sabbath*, Led Zeppelin had expanded their sound on *Houses of the Holy*, as did Budgie on the classics *Never Turn Your Back on a Friend* and *In for the Kill!* Meanwhile a little band called Queen had come along with the raucous *Sheer Heart Attack* and were about to put out the immortal *A Night at the Opera*.

However, no one, at least in the mainstream sphere, had yet to combine prog and nascent heavy metal. *Fly By Night* married those two styles, meshing the intricate musicianship of Yes and Genesis with the raw visceral power of Jeff Beck and Led Zeppelin. Gone were the overt homages to Cream and groovy jams: the band now sounded much tighter thanks to Neil's highly disciplined drumming; Lifeson's riffs sounded razor sharp and nimble; and Geddy's vocal melodies became more challenging and far less predictable. Like any other second record by a talented band, it was a transitional work, as Rush started to move far beyond the groundwork that the debut had laid. It's not a perfect record, but its giddy sense of discovery is irresistible.

Fittingly, *Fly By Night* opens with the cannonading "Anthem," a four-and-a-half-minute barrage of riffs, drum fills, and stops and starts that wastes no time declaring to one and all that this was a different band, one with a lot more ambition and a lot more to say than it had six months earlier. A crucial transitional moment in the band's development, "Anthem" would pave the way for a much bigger, visionary, career-altering composition a couple years later. And although it would come to epitomize the band's uncompromising attitude, the controversial source material from which it is derived would eventually land Peart in some hot water in the UK and Europe.

As soon as "Anthem" kicks in, listeners immediately hear how much different Rush sounds with the new drummer behind the kit, how the song has two intro sections, and how those two intros create a dramatic effect that acts as a perfect way to kick off this new chapter in the band's history. Initially those opening bars of "Anthem" feel overwhelming: Lifeson and Lee launch into a crazy riff sequence that defies logic: four insistent, ascending chords followed by a nimble series of staccato hammer-ons and pull-offs, repeated three times before returning to the beginning, and then wash, rinse, repeat. As Lifeson displays far more flash than he did on the entire first album, Peart punctuates every note Alex hits, his snare beats going into overdrive. In full Keith Moon mode, Peart throttles the hell out of his chrome-plated Slingerland kit, but what immediately sets his playing apart from the rest of rock drumming royalty is how taut his playing is. Every single beat is precisely on point. For a passage this intricately arranged, precision is a must, and Peart wastes no time showing not only his chops but his importance, his worth, in this power trio.

After five furiously paced repetitions of that overture progression, "Anthem" begins in earnest, Lifeson launching into a looser, gnarlier, downward sliding riff that feels like more of a gallop, and when he's joined by Geddy and Neil, the headbanging groove kicks in. A drummer like Rutsey would have drummed a little more behind the beat to let that riff breathe, but Peart's tighter playing allows him to propel the music forward. Seemingly overnight, the focal point in Rush quickly became the drums: the power and precision commands the listener's attention.

After those two memorable intros, Geddy dives into Peart's first verse, backed up by an understated, swinging arrangement that makes plenty of room for Neil's lyrics to grab listeners' attention. On the surface it feels as though "Anthem" is a run-of-the-mill self-empowerment treatise—a trope that would only get more popular among heavy metal bands for the next couple decades—but dig a little deeper into who and what inspired the song and things get more interesting.

Call Ayn Rand what you will: objectivist philosopher, mediocre writer, champion of selfishness, fascist, laissez-faire capitalist, libertarian, conservative, hero to everyone on the far right from CEOs to MAGA cultists to spoiled white males. Regardless of your opinion of Rand, it's easy to see how her work would have had an impact on a struggling young musician fighting tooth and nail to make a living in the brutal, often corrupt microverse that is the music industry.

Rand's 1938 novella *Anthem* and her 1943 novel *The Fountainhead* had a huge impact on the young Peart, who would have been around the same age as *Anthem*'s protagonist when he read it. *Anthem*'s plot is rigidly written, paranoid, libertarian propaganda: a twenty-one-year-old man named Equality 7-2521 lives in a dystopian communal society where everything a person does is done for the good of the collective, to the point where individuals are given numerical names and are referred to in the plural, while personal expression and free will are strictly stifled by the elders. Young Mr. Equality 7-2521 convinces himself he's been given the "curse" of being able to learn quickly and question things, discovers a tunnel leading to relics from the distant capitalist past, conducts illegal science experiments, falls for a teenaged girl named Liberty 5-3000, sees his "discovery" of electricity vehemently denounced by the elders, and runs away with his woman to live all alone and start populating the world with "individuals."

"To a 20-year-old struggling musician, *The Fountainhead* was a revelation, an affirmation, an inspiration," Peart wrote in his 2004 book *Traveling Music.* "Although I would eventually grow into and, largely, out of Ayn Rand's orbit, her writing was still a significant stepping-stone, or way-station, for me, a black-and-white starting point along the journey to a more nuanced philosophy and politics. Most of all, it was the notion of individualism that I needed—the idea that what I felt, believed, liked, and wanted was important and valid."

There's no denying Rand's individualistic stance could help motivate someone like Peart, and starting with Rush's song "Anthem," the band started to dig in their heels when it came to dealing with demands from the suits at Mercury Records in America. For the next few years, that idea of the individual's needs surpassing the good of the collective would play a massive role in Rush's own march toward artistic autonomy. They would do things their way, and if they failed and had to go back to their day jobs, then at least they tried.

The forcefulness of "Anthem's" lyrics is echoed brilliantly by a great little touch in the last line of the chorus when Geddy hollers the line as Peart punctuates the vocal cadence with monstrous yet fluid drum fills. It's the kind of stuff that instantly draws in any social misfit, catnip for introverted teenage boys in the mid-'70s, not to mention their older, weed-smoking siblings.

Structurally, "Anthem" is conventional, but thanks to Peart's presence and the trio's ferocity, the song brims with urgency, the sound of a hungry young band finding its voice. Just listen to how they close the song in its final thirty seconds, stopping and starting, hammering out E-chord couplets and drum thuds with all their might. It's all testosterone, ambition, and desperation, and while Rush would go on to write more complex and sophisticated music, "Anthem" is arguably the fiercest and heaviest moment in the entire discography.

Rand's influence on Peart and Rush would eventually fade, but not before the band's 1976 breakthrough side-long track "2112," whose storyline closely mirrors that of *Anthem* and which Peart dedicated "to the genius of Ayn Rand." By then Rush's name would be ascendant, and a genuinely concerned British music press would inevitably confront Peart with questions about why he chose to side with a fascist writer, especially considering the world warred against fascism for five harrowing years three decades prior. Writing for the *New Musical Express* in 1978, Barry Miles was scathing in his indictment of Rush: "They are actually very nice guys. They don't sit there in jackboots pulling the wings off flies. They are polite, charming even, naïve—roaming the concert circuits preaching what to me seems like proto-fascism like a leper without a bell."

Geddy Lee eloquently told *Paste* magazine in 2015, "[Rand's] point of individualism was more appropriate and influential in terms of compromise as an artist. . . . When you're a young band that's in a greedy business like the music business, and there's so much pressure on you to compromise your music and write three-minute love songs, when you read a book like that it has a profound effect on you in terms of reinforcing your belief that it should be about making the music you want to make, and not the music someone else wants you to make in order to line their pockets."

Peart, meanwhile, would gradually drift away from Rand's teachings and embrace the idea of the greater good while at the same time humbly enjoying the luxury of being able to live strictly on his own terms. Speaking with *Rolling Stone* in 2012, he said, "[Rand] was important to me at the time in a transition of finding myself and having faith that what I believed was worthwhile. . . . As you go through past your twenties, your idealism is going to be disappointed many, many times. . . . Libertarianism as I understood it was very good and pure and we're all going to be successful and generous to the less fortunate and it was, to me, not dark or cynical. But then I soon saw, of course, the way that it gets twisted by the flaws of humanity. And that's when I evolve now into . . . a bleeding-heart libertarian. That'll do."

Chapter Two Playlist:

"Sing, Sing, Sing," Gene Krupa

"Chains," The Cookies

"Hold On, I'm Comin'," Sam & Dave

"Close to the Edge," Yes

"Firth of Fifth," Genesis

"Karn Evil 9 1st Impression, Part 2," Emerson, Lake & Palmer

"The Song Remains the Same," Led Zeppelin

"Red," King Crimson

"On the Run," Pink Floyd

"Who Are You?," Black Sabbath

"Brighton Rock," Queen

3

"XANADU"

The Epic Years

On December 29, 1977, Rush kicked off a two-night residency at Toronto's Maple Leaf Gardens, which, for these local boys, was their biggest achievement as a band yet. By then they had five studio albums (and one live album) under their belts, the most recent of which, *A Farewell to Kings*, cracked the Billboard Top 40 for the first time, peaking at 33. That record's first single, a stately, English-folk-tinged tune called "Closer to the Heart," made it to number 36 in the UK. Rush were now headlining arenas, and this era produced the most iconic Rush images, what people still envision when they hear the name: long, flowing hair, Neil Peart's ostentatious moustache, their garish silk kimonos, Peart's perpetually expanding drum kit—now with tubular bells, glockenspiel, wind chimes, temple blocks, timbales, bell tree, triangles, and melodic cowbells—and best of all, the two lavish double-necked guitars that Geddy Lee and Alex Lifeson would play. The music had also expanded, as the band incorporated synthesizers and bass pedals to help maximize what this trio could do onstage. Coupled with their reputation for epic, labyrinthine tales of fantasy and science fiction, Rush captured the imaginations of millions of teenaged listeners, who flocked to the shows. And to think, less than two years earlier Rush's future was in major jeopardy thanks to a third album that was a commercial and critical failure.

Rush was justifiably confident after the small groundswell of success thanks to 1975's *Fly By Night*. Peart's presence behind the kit added a valuable new dimension to the band's sound, and his vivid imagination gave the band the lyricist they so badly needed. As mentioned in the previous chapter, that album's track "Anthem" was an early turning point in their development, but "By-Tor and the Snow Dog" is also a key moment, in which Rush started to display an acumen for lengthier, more ambitious compositions.

An early example of Peart's irreverent sense of humor, "By-Tor and the Snow Dog" took its inspiration from two dogs owned by Ray Danniels, one a German shepherd, the other a white Husky. After the shepherd tried to bite lighting manager Howard Ungerleider, Peart punnily renamed the pup "By-Tor" and then came up with a whimsical fantasy involving a battle between two hounds of Hell. With Danniels's husky aptly named "Snow Dog," Peart, Lee, and Lifeson conjured up a lively, eight-and-a-half-minute, eight-movement suite that depicted the dogs as mighty forces of evil: Snow Dog crosses the River Styx to do battle with Prince By-Tor at the Tobes of Hades, and mayhem ensues. The "battle" section of the song features a clever and very fun duel between

Lifeson and Lee, whose solos symbolize the blows between the combatants, the violence accentuated by a rousing drum solo by Peart. For a first attempt at an epic progressive rock song, it's an auspicious moment for the young, developing band.

Recorded months after *Fly By Night* hit record stores and released on September 24, 1975, *Caress of Steel* was supposed to be the breakthrough third album the band, management, and record execs expected. All the ingredients were there: a driven young band that was an absolute force onstage, a continual desire to expand and evolve their increasingly distinctive sound, a talented lyricist, and plenty of positive word of mouth thanks to two years of near-constant touring. Like a young baseball phenom whose eyes grow huge at the sight of a hanging slider, Rush swung for the fences, connected, and . . . popped out to the shortstop.

Caress of Steel bombed. Badly. "I played the latest (and admittedly rather derivative) Rush album *Caress of Steel* in the office the other day, and unfortunately it received howls of derision," wrote Geoff Barton for *Sounds* magazine at the time. The record was lambasted by critics, or those who bothered to listen to it, and fared worse commercially, peaking at 60 in Canada and, even worse, an abysmal 148 in the United States. It would take another eighteen years to be certified gold in America, signifying five hundred thousand copies sold. Much to the band's chagrin, the steel-like, silver-inked cover artwork by Hugh Syme—his first Rush cover in what would turn out to be a long and fruitful creative partnership—came back from the presses looking more of a dark gold . . . or, more fittingly, rust.

It's frustrating because the energy, ambition, and musicianship are all there, but only two short songs, nine minutes of the album's entire forty-five-minute running time, work. Opener "Bastille Day" is an early Rush classic, a thunderous depiction of the French Revolution that would become a live staple for years. Meanwhile, "Lakeside Park" is a wistful, acoustic-driven song that sees Peart reminiscing about growing up in Ontario's pastoral Niagara region.

The rest of the album fails outright. "I Think I'm Going Bald" has a very funny backstory: it's both a parody of "Goin' Blind" by their good friends and touring pals Kiss, as well as a playful poke at Alex's continual fretting about whether or not he was losing his hair. Sadly, the song's attempt at Frank Zappa–style humor falls woefully flat.

More troubling, though, are the two epic compositions that comprise the album's final half hour. Following the creative breakthroughs "Anthem" and "By-Tor and the Snow Dog" a year earlier, Rush attempted more ambitious material as the next obvious step. On the twelve-and-a-half-minute, Tolkien-inspired "The Necromancer" and the twenty-minute fantasy "The Fountain of Lamneth," the trio pulls out all the stops, and while there are sections of each song that bring a few impressive moments, none of it gels.

"The Necromancer" is a hot mess. It starts with a drowsy, lifeless narration by a pitch-shifted Peart, sleepwalks through a mellow extended section ("Into the Darkness"), wakes up halfway through with a pretty damned wicked Sabbath-style jam that carries on for four and a half minutes ("Under the Shadow"), and then—incomprehensibly—shifts into a jam that shamelessly rips off the Velvet Underground's 1970 song "Sweet Jane" ("Return of the Prince," by far the strangest radio single Rush ever released). There's no fluidity at all.

"The Fountain of Lamneth," which takes up all of side two, fares better, tied together by a stuttering riff that recurs throughout the song. Unfortunately, after the raucous minute-long "Didacts and Narpets" section (featuring a fun drum solo by Peart) the momentum grinds to a halt thanks to the eleven-minute slog that is "No One at the Bridge," "Panacea," and "Bacchus Plateau." It isn't until the sixteen-minute mark when the song wakes up and charges toward a long-awaited conclusion.

Spirits were so low on the late-1975 tour in support of *Caress of Steel* that the band and crew took to calling it the "Down the Tubes Tour." The boys started to wonder if this was the end of the road for Rush, and Lifeson even started mentally planning to return to helping his father's plumbing business. Despite gentle reassurances from manager Danniels, there was reason to worry that Mercury would drop Rush from its US roster. Both management and label were steadfast in their belief that the next record had to be considerably more accessible than *Caress*. The band decided, however, that if they were going to go down, they'd go down in flames, completely on their own terms.

In response to Mercury's request for more radio-friendly songs, Rush delivered a fourth album with a sidelong conceptual piece as the opening track. Label executives were baffled by what they heard, but by early 1976, Rush was such a low priority that Mercury didn't even include the band in its financial forecasts for that year. Danniels saw that as an opportunity to tour hard in support of the record, specifically targeting the young, rapidly growing heavy metal audience. After all, when the label has so little faith in you that they don't care what you do at this point, why not go all out? To quote Kiss, you got nothin' to lose.

Released in the spring of 1976, *2112* succeeded in every way that *Caress of Steel* failed. At nearly twenty-one minutes, the epic title track is a triumph of composition, concept, musicianship, and production. The band clearly learned what was missing from *Caress of Steel*, as "2112" is much tighter, much more cohesive, and best of all, tells a genuinely engaging story, holding the listener riveted for the song's entirety. Brazenly copping the concept from Ayn Rand's *Anthem* and *The Fountainhead*, Peart's story can easily be read as an allegory for Rush's own struggles against a major label.

In the program for Rush's three-night residency at Toronto's Massey Hall—which yielded the ferocious live album *All the World's a Stage*—fans were treated to a small libretto explaining the concept of "2112":

> In the year 2062, a galaxy-wide war results in the union of all planets under the rule of the Red Star of the Solar Federation. The world is controlled by computers, called Temples,

which determine all reading matter, songs, pictures . . . every-thing connected with life during the year 2112.

In the midst of this assembly line living, a man discovers what was once known years before as a guitar ("Discovery"). The man begins to pluck the strings and turn the knobs, dis-covering that he can make his own—a music much different than that of the Temples. He rushes to tell the priests of his discovery ("Presentation"), but to the man's dismay, the priests dismiss the instrument, saying it doesn't fit the plan of the Solar Federation.

The man returns to the cave in which he found the gui-tar and, during a dream, is led by an oracle to a land of incredible beauty and serenity ("Oracle: A Dream"). Upon awakening, he cannot believe it was a dream—the beauty was so real.

He remains in the cave for several days, becoming more and more depressed with each passing hour ("Soliloquy"). The man decides he cannot go on as part of the Federation and takes his life to move on to a better one. As he dies, another planetary battle begins ("Grand Finale") with the outcome to be determined in the mind of the listener.

Similar to "Anthem," the Rand-inspired theme of "2112" works because Rush themselves were in their own existential battle with a label that had all but written them off. Better yet, Peart's much-improved lyric writing is backed up by a highly dynamic instrumental arrangement that not only illustrates the storyline but drives it. Lee, Lifeson, and Peart are on fire, starting with the monumental "Overture," allowing the music to ebb and flow just like the plot. Lee turns in an astonishing vocal performance, adopting an innocent singing voice for the main character and a piercing scream when singing from the elders' point of view. Lifeson comes into his own as a lead guitarist, effectively capturing the innocence of "Discovery," wrenching soulful, anguished notes during "Soliloquy," and leading the charge during the rampaging final movement that brings the song to an apocalyptic end, Peart's commanding voice booming over the crescendo: "Attention all planets of the Solar Federation: we have assumed control."

2112 saved Rush's career. While the album's second half is itself very good (stoner anthem "A Passage to Bangkok," "Twilight Zone," and "Something for Nothing" remain underrated tracks), it was the title track that captured the imaginations of young heavy music fans, particularly those who loved fantasy and sci-fi. The album peaked at number 60 in America, reached the top 5 in Canada, and more impressively, had outsold Rush's previous three albums combined by June 1976.

While everything fell into place on *2112*, those pieces coalesced gracefully on *A Farewell to Kings*. It was recorded at Rockfield Studios in Wales in June 1977 and released that September. Lee, Lifeson, and Peart took full advantage of the quaint, pastoral surroundings. Lifeson would record some acoustic guitar passages outside with birds twittering in the background, and similar ambience echoes throughout the album, be it field recordings or studio replications. UK progressive rock was still doing well despite punk rock capturing the music media's attention—Camel, Van der Graaf Generator, U.K., and standard-bearers Pink Floyd were stalwarts of the late 1970s—and *A Farewell to Kings* comfortably fits alongside Rush's British peers.

Opening and closing side one are two gorgeous singles that are beloved by fans. The title track is a seamless mélange of classical guitar, gentle Moog synths, glockenspiel, and a grandiose explosion of twelve-string electric guitars that chime out a stately riff that feels immediately pleasing to the ear. One of Rush's most enduring and endearing tracks, "Closer to the Heart" channels traditional English folk music in sublime fashion, its timeless melody and tubular bell accents conveying a sense of warmth that the band had never pulled off before. It's the song in the middle of side one, however, that remains one of the band's finest achievements.

At eleven minutes, "Xanadu" is nowhere near as long as "2112," nor is it as iconic in popular culture, but it does capture Rush at their most musically curious. It flows so much better than "2112," it says a lot more with much less, and the lengths the threesome would go to expand their sound without adding additional musicians would further validate what Metallica's Kirk Hammett would famously say a few decades later: "How could three people make such a sound?"

"In 1975 I was trying to write a song inspired by the dark mood and subtle psychology of the film *Citizen Kane*, which features the opening lines of 'Kubla Khan' by Samuel Taylor Coleridge," Peart told *The Guardian* in 2010. "I looked up the poem and was overwhelmed by its imagery and emotional power. The song 'Xanadu' was taken over by the poem in a way that has never happened since. . . . I portrayed Coleridge's idea of immortality as a grim curse—*Citizen Kane* is the opposite: mortality as a punishment."

Written in 1797 after Coleridge woke up in the middle of an opium-fueled dream, "Xanadu" is one of the poet's most spellbinding works, a short but vivid depiction of humankind's perpetual quest for beauty and immortality, how man-made pleasure can never equal the beauty of nature itself. By building his perfect "pleasure-dome," Kubla Khan deprives himself of the awe-inspiring beauty of nature. To Coleridge, the only "dome" humanity needs is the sky above.

Peart approaches this subject with great imagination. His narrator strives to achieve immortality by searching for Kubla Khan's fabled Xanadu. When the explorer finds Xanadu, Peart writes a marvelous verse that deftly quotes imagery from the original poem (the River Alph, caves of ice, honeydew, milk of paradise) but rearranges it all to fit the perspective of the protagonist's narrative.

And whaddya know, immortality turns out to be not so great after all. Living forever would drive anyone mad, and during the song's final passages, we rejoin our subject a thousand years later. He's exhausted, frozen, staring at a lifeless sky, waiting for it all to finally end, wishing for the lost paradise/prison Xanadu.

When Peart reprises the first refrain, he rewrites it from the perspective of the now insane narrator, who realizes that he might want to be careful about what he wishes for. Sometimes a fantasy is best left a fantasy. And frankly, melon with a milk chaser isn't all it's cracked up to be.

The musicianship on Rush's "Xanadu" is a wonder, starting with the opening instrumental section, which finds the band excelling at what's commonly known as "program music," a classical music technique that peaked in popularity during the nineteenth century thanks to such composers as Richard Strauss and Camille Saint-Saëns. Essentially, program music provides an extramusical narrative to the overall composition, a way of setting the scene using traditional instrumentation in defiantly nontraditional ways, creating atmosphere rather than delivering a melody.

Rush had dabbled in program music on "2112," most notably in the "Discovery" movement, where Lifeson depicts the main character picking up a guitar, tinkering with it, slowly tuning it, and eventually playing a chord. In "Xanadu" all three members of Rush take part, and coupled with more recordings of those twittering Welsh birds, the effect is sublime. Lee starts off with an understated drone sound from his mini-Moog as Lifeson first echoes the drone on guitar before playing gentle swells. Peart, meanwhile, enters with temple block notes that mimic water drops, and as Lifeson's swells steadily create a small melody, Peart responds with tubular bell chimes. After the fourth chime, Lifeson enters with a 7/8 melody that repeats, gradually building intensity, punctuated by some truly gorgeous fills by Peart.

After the intro and overture, around the three-minute mark, the traditional power trio arrangement begins with a pensive melody driven by Lee's upper-register bassline and Peart's lively drumming. So begins a thrilling final seven minutes of the song that sees Rush displaying the most versatility to date. Peart switches from bell tree to tubular bells to furious beats on a full kit, all on a dime. Lee plays synthesizer while playing the bassline on Taurus pedals, then switches seamlessly to electric bass, not to mention nailing a very challenging vocal melody. Interestingly, it's Lifeson who anchors the song, alternating between texture, powerful chords, and evocative solos.

"Xanadu" also conjures that memorable image of Geddy and Alex onstage playing their own double-necked guitars: Lifeson's a Gibson EDS-1275 Doubleneck with a twelve-string and six-string guitar, Lee's a Rickenbacker 4080 Doubleneck with four-string bass and six-string guitar. The double-necked dexterity peaks immediately following the final refrain. First, Lifeson strums a plaintive twelve-string riff backed by Peart's bells and Lee's Moog, and without missing a beat he switches to an ominous, Sabbath-esque string-bent riff on the six-string neck. Lee, meanwhile, switches deftly from synth to his own six-string neck, playing rhythm guitar as well as the bassline with his foot pedals, supporting Lifeson's bluesy solo.

At the song's climax, Lifeson reprises the seven-note riff from the overture, which then deconstructs itself into a hushed, minimalist conclusion. All three members—Lee and Lifeson on guitar, Peart on glockenspiel—gel neatly, each playing the same gentle melody as the listener absorbs the moral of the story.

Singing about such heady topics as eighteenth-century poetry did make Rush targets of playful teasing by their tourmates in the hard rock scene, most notably British greats UFO. Rush and UFO made a highly unlikely pairing, considering the Canadians were polite, mellow guys who enjoyed weed, prog, and literature while the Brits were some of the most intense and chaotic partiers hard rock has ever seen. But both bands became great friends, and UFO loved to have fun at the expense of the Rush boys, especially when it came to "Xanadu" and the silk kimonos they wore onstage during this period.

In the 2017 memoir by UFO's late, great bassist Pete Way, Geddy speaks at length about their friendship. "We used to play the song 'Xanadu' at the time, and yes, all kinds of dry ice would come on stage. Pete and [UFO singer] Phil Mogg would stand at the side of the stage and yell things about honeydew and melons at us, because one of the lines in the song goes 'I have dined on honeydew.' On one occasion, they even snuck up on stage and nailed a pair of slippers beside my foot pedals. There the slippers were when the dry ice dissipated, I guess to go along with my kimono."

In his autobiography, Way wrote, "I would go round to Geddy's house whenever we were in Toronto. I would have our tour bus park at the end of his road and used to move all the bloody awful Yes albums from the front to the back of his record collection."

Another, much darker themed progressive rock epic would conclude *A Farewell to Kings*. A sci-fi conceptual piece about a spaceship careening toward a black hole, "Cygnus X-1 Book I: The Voyage" would send Rush into a creative black hole of their own making. As bleak, menacing, and enthralling as the composition is, it suffers from not being as immediately accessible as "Xanadu." Peart's dense storyline keeps listeners at an arm's length, and there are fewer melodic hooks to hold people's attention. It's a grower, no question, and the more you delve into the track, the more fascinating it becomes, especially during its murky, almost apocalyptic second half as the narrator's ship, the *Rocinante*, is sent spiraling into the mighty black hole.

"The Voyage" would become a particular favorite of Rush's most fervent '70s prog fans—and it was indeed a thrill to see the band revisit it on their final tour in 2015—but by calling it "Book 1" they had painted themselves into a corner. It was obvious that the next record would require a "Book 2," or else they'd never hear the end of it from fans, so there was immediate pressure to make the sequel even bigger, more complex, and more exciting than ever before.

Chapter Three Playlist:

"Xanadu" (*A Farewell to Kings*), Rush
"Bastille Day" (*All the World's a Stage*), Rush
"2112," Rush

"Dogs," Pink Floyd

"Song within a Song," Camel

"Childlike Faith in Childhood's End," Van der Graaf Generator

"In the Dead of Night," U.K.

"Lights Out," UFO

"A Farewell to Kings," Rush

"Cygnus X-1," Rush

"Xanadu" (*Exit . . . Stage Left*), Rush

4

"THE SPIRIT OF RADIO"

Reinvention

In 1980 a television reporter asked Rush if their new album *Permanent Waves* was a deliberate attempt to strip down their sound to keep up with the more minimal style of the emerging new wave bands at the time. Geddy Lee replied, "Some bands have gone back to basics, but those are the bands that can't do anything but play the basics. All the real interesting new wave bands seem to be developing and progressing into more interesting styles."

Progressive rock is supposed to progress, not regress. By the end of the 1970s, Rush felt that their music was progressing in the wrong direction. Yes, they were getting more popular with every new release, but one look at the crowd at a Rush concert in the 1970s would tell you that the vast majority of their audience fell under a startlingly narrow demographic: teenaged, white, and overwhelmingly male.

Today it's odd to consider how binary rock music in the 1970s and 1980s really was. And Rush were hardly the most overtly masculine rock band out there: they loved to learn, they read a lot, they didn't indulge in groupies, and they wore those fancy kimonos onstage. Still, sad as it looks in retrospect, sci-fi themed rock music with heavy riffs and labyrinthine arrangements played by three guys who weren't exactly as pretty as Robert Plant attracted a disproportionate number of white males. It was never Rush's intention, but for the longest time they were largely—but not completely—a boys' club (that "only white guys like Rush" trope was satirized brilliantly, and endearingly, in the 2009 bromance comedy *I Love You, Man*). For all the strides that were made during the post–civil rights era, cross-pollination in contemporary music just didn't happen a lot.

The media's approach to popular music didn't exactly foster diversity, either. Black audiences had soul and R&B. The gay crowd had disco. In middle America (or non-urban Canada, for that matter), there wasn't much access to either sound, at least before disco blew up with *Saturday Night Fever* in 1978. Pop and rock on AM radio was geared primarily toward white women, while album-oriented rock on FM, the only format where Rush received regular airplay, attracted a predominantly male crowd. With the channels of music distribution so narrow, it was a lot harder than it is today to expose oneself to the real diversity of music. So radio listeners became accustomed to what their demographic was fed.

Kids in predominantly white places like Des Moines, Madison, and Winnipeg usually had a choice between top 40, country, or AOR (if they were lucky enough to have an FM station) and it wouldn't be until punk rock and new wave flipped the tables in the late '70s that the public started to develop an appetite for much broader, diverse music. In their dogged pursuit of their own musical interests, Rush didn't realize until 1978 that they had painted themselves into a corner.

When all you're doing is trying to one-up your previous album in complexity, that well will quickly run dry, and the band started to feel it during the writing and recording of *Hemispheres*, the 1978 follow-up to the successful *A Farewell to Kings*. By the end of the summer of 1978, Lee, Lifeson, and Peart were all but finished with their 1970s brand of epic progressive rock and eager to change Rush's direction.

That's not to say that *Hemispheres* isn't a good album. Far from it. It's a beloved record among Rush fans and the pinnacle of that era of the band's history. *Rolling Stone* magazine even ranked it thirteenth in their list of the greatest progressive rock albums of all time. All the ideas Rush embraced in the 1970s—combining nascent heavy metal with more experimental, conceptual touches to create something dizzying yet imaginative and accessible—were captured beautifully on *Hemispheres*.

Ironically, for a record that's emblematic of Rush at their technically headiest, it's shockingly economical, running at a crisp thirty-six minutes. Just like *2112*, *Hemispheres* opens with a side-long composition, the eighteen-minute "Cygnus X-1 Book II: Hemispheres." On side two, "Circumstances" is a streamlined rocker, while the more acoustic-leaning "The Trees" is another

Ayn Rand–derived allegory by Peart in which maples quarrel with oaks because the taller oaks are hogging the sunlight. Although it's one of Peart's more heavy-handed songs, the arrangement and the musicianship—dig Peart's magnificent utilization of wooden temple blocks—make up for the fact that the song's basically depicting, for all the Tolkien fans out there, a libertarian Entmoot. Instrumental "La Villa Strangiato," on the other hand, features Rush at their most playful, a wild nine-and-a-half-minute ride that whips the listener from classical guitar to pastoral-sounding prog, to jazz fusion, to an inspired quotation of Raymond Scott's "Powerhouse." It's all a bit nuts, but Rush's mastery of discipline and dynamics prevents the song from flying off the rails.

Hemispheres is great fun for listeners, but it sure as hell was anything but fun for Rush. Recorded at the same Welsh studio where *A Farewell to Kings* was made, the idea to use the same method that worked so well the year before backfired badly. The three-week songwriting process quickly devolved into an around-the-clock slog with no time off, the band digging themselves a deeper and deeper hole as their new material flirted with becoming too unwieldy to pull off on record. The trio was so far down the prog rabbit hole that they could no longer see the forest for all those darned oaks and maples in the way.

Just how bad did things get? The writing and arranging had taken so long that the band left the recording of the vocal tracks to the very last, after all the instrumental tracks were laid down. They were so wrapped up in fine-tuning the arrangements that they didn't realize that "Hemispheres" was in a key too high for Geddy to sing. "Geddy had a few hissy fits and got upset," producer Terry Brown told musicologist Rob Bowman. "He was pissed off at everybody including himself. It was a little tense. I remember Ged throwing his arms in the air in the studio and going, 'I can't fucking sing these songs. This hurts!' and getting mad. [I said], 'Well, we're gonna do this so you might as well get used to it.'"

"It felt like the end of an era for me," Lee told *Classic Rock* magazine in 2021. "I felt that the side-long [songs] thing was getting predictable for me as a writer, and I wanted to bust out of that. In a sense it felt like saying goodbye to that period. I had ideas of where I wanted us to go. Songs like 'The Trees' and 'Circumstances' pointed in that direction. I wanted to tell stories, but I didn't want to be weighed down by themes that had to keep repeating over a twenty-five-minute period."

The trio was increasingly absorbing new influences from outside the classic rock realm, which by the end of the 1970s was sounding toothless in comparison to the new generation of artists emerging in the wake of punk rock. Two bands in particular had an enormous influence on Lifeson and Peart, and would help steer Rush in a happier and more artistically rewarding direction at the dawn of the new decade.

Evoking both the glam rock of Roxy Music and the politically charged anger of the punk scene, London's Ultravox scored a few minor hits in the UK before changing direction on their pivotal 1978 album. Produced by Krautrock legend Conny Plank, *Systems of Romance* anticipated the early-'80s New Romantic sound by combining cutting-edge synthesizers with wiry, textured guitar work on such landmark tracks as "Slow Motion" and "I Can't Stay Long." Peart loved the economy and emotional power of the music, while Lifeson was drawn to the less riff-oriented sound of the guitars, and when Midge Ure joined Ultravox as singer/guitarist in time for 1980's classic *Vienna*, Peart and Lifeson were wowed.

Budding British superstars the Police had a similarly massive impact on Peart and Lifeson. Cleverly incorporating/appropriating reggae, punk, jazz, worldbeat, and new age into a very pop-friendly package, the Police boasted a musical pedigree that few bands of the late '70s could match. Gordon "Sting" Sumner had a background in jazz bass as well as punk, drummer Stewart Copeland played in the great prog band Curved Air and had a minimalist yet powerful drumming style, and guitarist Andy Summers was a veteran musician who had played with the Animals and Soft Machine. They were a phenomenal, highly combustible trio who, like Rush, boasted jaw-dropping musical proficiency, and the albums *Outlandos d'Amour* and *Regatta de Blanc* combined directness and texture in a way that Peart and Lifeson found tantalizing. The 1979 single "Walking on the Moon" alone contains many moments that foreshadow what Rush would do between 1980 and 1984.

Geddy Lee, meanwhile, was having fun learning how to integrate keyboards, bass pedals, and bass guitar into his live repertoire, which in turn profoundly informed how Rush would write their seventh album. Lee would tell *Guitar Player* in 1980, "It was a real education, and my all-around musical sense really had a shot in the arm because I could listen to things and write from a different perspective. So, rather than just write a bass riff, I could think in terms of composing a melody. I'd go over to the synthesizer and work out a melody, transpose that to bass, and have a more interesting bass line to work with. And coordinating my bass work with a foot pedal sound makes the rhythm section a whole lot more complete."

Those new musical influences, combined with Geddy's new approach to his own role in the band and the desire to escape the corner they'd painted themselves into on *Hemispheres*, paved the way for 1980's *Permanent Waves*, Rush's most radical creative statement to date. The entire process—writing, rehearsing, recording—was the opposite of the miserable experience that was the making of *Hemispheres*. Instead of uprooting to Wales for several months, Rush stayed closer to home, booking a stay at Le Studio, located in the Laurentian Mountains in rural Quebec, in the fall of 1979. The mood was immediately lighter in the quiet, woodsy setting, and the change of pace was the perfect way for the band to tap into their growing musical curiosity.

Suddenly, instinctively, Rush's sound expanded yet shrunk at the same time. There was more breadth to the arrangements and a lot more space for ideas to breathe. Melodies became simpler, the music was less reliant on the heavy rock riff, and keyboards and less overdriven guitars opened up the sound a lot more. Peart's drumming started to simplify, and most importantly, his lyrics moved from straightforward storytelling to something more observational and philosophical. And crucially for Lee, because his vocal tracks were so arduous on the last record, he started writing vocal melodies that were lower in register, making it far more comfortable for him to sing. In so doing, his less-shrieky vocals made Rush's new music even more palatable to mass audiences.

There was no better song for Rush to usher in the 1980s with than the first song on side one of *Permanent Waves*. One of Rush's most universally beloved songs—right up there with "Tom Sawyer" and "Limelight"—"The Spirit of Radio" might seem like a simpler track because of its heavy reliance on melody rather than complexity, but when listened to closely, it is a perfect distillation of everything the band was excelling at around that time. With a couple new ideas tossed in for good measure.

For a song that's a classic rock radio staple, "The Spirit of Radio" was initially inspired by one of the only Canadian radio stations to play Rush's music in the 1970s. Originally darlings of FM radio back when it was more of a free-form, disc-jockey-curated format, times were changing quickly as FM started to focus more on the commercial, mainstream side of rock and pop music.

"We were working at a farmhouse out in the country in western Ontario and commuting home on weekends," Peart said at the time. "I remember coming home very late and CFNY Radio was on the air as I was cresting the escarpment with all of the lights below of Hamilton and the Niagara Peninsula, where I lived at the time, with a fantastic combination of music that was on at the time."

And the station's catchphrase in 1979? "The spirit of radio."

Before going further, listen to just the first thirty-five seconds of the song. That extended intro feels like an extension of "La Villa Strangiato," the instrumental that closed *Hemispheres*. It's just as playful, just as complex. The opening lick by Lifeson is a very clever imagining of radio static, immediately catching the listener's attention, delivered as a series of fluid hammer-ons and pull-offs—where the bulk of the notes is made by the fret hand rather than the pick hand—its lilting melody almost sounding Celtic in influence.

Then the real fun begins, as Lee and Lifeson join in with fills that sound natural but are extremely difficult to replicate, or even to transcribe for that matter. People love to air drum to Rush, but even when miming at a school or office desk with a couple of ball-point pens in hand, it takes a long time to nail (trust me, I'm one of those people). The reason: measure seven of the intro shifts from 4/4 to 5/4 time, before returning to 4/4 in measure eight. It's a cheeky move, and brilliant, because it makes the listener instinctively think, what the hell? before continuing onward. And it takes some honest-to-goodness chemistry between the bassist and the drummer to nail these highly dexterous syncopations; consider how Lee's bassline has to match exactly with Peart's fills. There was no better rock rhythm section than Lee and Peart, and both are locked in, hitting the beats with precision.

After that intricate opening section, the band launch into a much more relaxed, swinging, gently ascending 6/8 heavy rock riff reminiscent of their mid-'70s work, but after four repetitions the song again shifts gears into an upbeat 4/4 groove that takes listeners into the heart of the matter. Lifeson plays gliding, chiming arpeggios, while Lee drives the main riff with his melodic bassline and Peart energizes the music with nimble ride cymbal beats. Geddy's voice finally enters, but it's different than before: it's still an upper-register tone, but it's gentler, less bombastic, less shrieking. He sounds welcoming, and the way he leans on the vowel sounds of the opening lines achieves the same effect as iambic pentameter, drawing the listener in as he sings Neil's vivid lyrics about how good music on the radio can add color to a person's otherwise monochrome workday.

Coming on the heels of the proggiest prog album Rush ever progged, to hear two simple verses atop such a gentle, ebullient groove is a breath of fresh air, but just then Rush pulls the rug out with another substantial shift, this time a bridge that features the most significant moment in the band's evolution to date.

It might sound primitive today, but the melodic, metronomic sequencer pattern that builds the structure of the song's chorus was a huge advancement for Rush, which would kick off a decade of experimentation with all things electronic. In "The Spirit of Radio," that sequencer adds a little touch of modernity to the band's rock foundation and helps enhance the radio theme: the sequencer taps along digitally, Peart mirrors the sequencer with glockenspiel, and Lifeson returns to his distinctive opening "radio wave" flourish. It's simple, and it's magical, as Lee waxes rhapsodic about crackling airwaves, bristling antennae, and emotional feedback.

Insisting on playing everything as a trio, with no backing musicians whatsoever, it was a challenge for Rush to work out just how to play this section of "The Spirit of Radio" live, but of course, they showed plenty of ingenuity. "In past years, we used sequencers for the sequenced parts in songs like 'New World Man' or 'Spirit of Radio,'" guitar/keyboard tech Jack Secret told *EQ* magazine in 1997. "When we started using the Roland S770 samplers, we discovered that we could record and loop sequences and trigger them in real time. . . . While you might think this sounds pretty easy, remember that if the sample is played late or early, it sounds (for its duration) out of time with the band. . . . So it really is critical for the band to trigger those samples exactly when they're supposed to start."

After that marvelous little section, the song returns to the previous arrangement, but although the melody is still bright, the lyrical tone shifts as Peart expresses despair at the growing commerciality and homogeneity of commercial radio, which as we all know has only gotten worse over time. It's the key moment in the song, a sudden realization that the best days of radio are already in the past. DJs don't program music anymore, and cynicism has replaced romanticism, a medium centered on humanity's love of music crassly turned into nothing more than a soulless form of advertising and corporate homogenization.

Instead of utilizing a guitar solo after the second chorus—as traditional rock songwriting usually dictates—Lee plays another upbeat melody, this time using his Taurus pedals, foreshadowing Lifeson's increasingly less prominent presence, which we'll get to in a couple chapters. The trio then returns to the tricky syncopation of the intro and that fun, swinging groove before throwing in another surprise— the fourth or fifth in a five-minute song—and this one's a doozy.

As Axl Rose once famously screamed, "Give us some reggae!" Here's the Police influence rearing its head, complete with subtle touches of steel drum. Already a popular style of music among Jamaican communities in the UK, reggae grew in popularity in the underground music scenes, and the Police cleverly appropriated the sound into their own music. Consequently, reggae suddenly became de rigueur among white rock fans, so for Rush to include a little reggae in 1980 was very of its time. And frankly, it works brilliantly in "The Spirit of Radio," especially at this crucial moment in the song, where Peart delivers one of his most mercifully cutting lines, cleverly paraphrasing Simon and Garfunkel's "The Sound of Silence," matter-of-factly admitting there's no escaping the unholy marriage of music and commerce, replacing "silence" with "salesmen."

Or, as Geddy famously cries, "SAYLES-men!"

After a welcome, wah-wah-enhanced solo by Lifeson and one more reprise of that swing riff, the song comes to a crisp, tight conclusion with a muted cymbal by Peart. For something so structurally complex, "The Spirit of Radio" feels so natural, so weirdly pleasant emanating from such a theoretically heady band. All the work of the previous decade led to this moment, where everything they learned could be worked into a concise, radio-friendly song that could fit on a seven-inch single.

And that single did very well, too, peaking on the UK charts at 13 (as mentioned, the Brits loved their reggae in 1980), at 22 in Canada, and at an impressive 51 in America. The song's legacy has only grown over the decades, immediately becoming one of Rush's calling cards.

Ironically, to this day commercial radio likes to play "The Spirit of Radio" as a tribute to how great they claim their deteriorating, algorithm-driven format still is. Every National Radio Day, classic rock stations boastfully blast the song with no regard for its deeper message, distracted by the upbeat melody and catchy hooks. As withering a statement as Neil Peart's lyrics are, the way the message continues to be lost on corporate radio as they still play the song makes the satire even more effective.

Meanwhile, the rest of *Permanent Waves* is often just as strong as its lead single. Another Peart exercise in Randian individualism, the defiantly atheist single "Freewill" became another big fan favorite thanks to its direct, Philosophy 101 approach ("You can choose a ready guide in some celestial voice / If you choose not to decide, you still have made a choice"). However, three deeper cuts antici- pate the darker, more observational tone of *Moving Pictures*. French for the phrase "between us," the tender "Entre Nous" sees Peart eschew storytelling for rumination, musing profoundly about the different ways human beings connect with one another ("I think it's time for us to realize / The spaces in between / Leave room for you and I to grow"). The haunting "Jacob's Ladder" is even simpler, built around Peart's reaction to the sun breaking through storm clouds, while "Natural Science" sees Neil contemplating the tiny universes in a single tidal pool.

So confident in this new direction was Rush that—at the suggestion of Mercury's Cliff Burnstein—they shelved a live album recorded on the *Permanent Waves* tour in favor of heading back to Le Studio merely nine months after the album's January 1980 release to sustain this positive momentum. Just like the decision to write and record *2112* five years earlier, the gambit would change the threesome's lives.

Chapter Four Playlist:

"La Villa Strangiato," Rush

"Slow Motion," Ultravox

"I Can't Stay Long," Ultravox

"Walking on the Moon," The Police

"(White Man) in Hammersmith Palais," The Clash

"Gangsters," The Specials

"The Spirit of Radio," Rush

"The Sound of Silence," Simon & Garfunkel

"The Spirit of Radio," Selina Martin

"Jacob's Ladder," Rush

"The Spirit of Radio" (*Exit . . . Stage Left*), Rush

5

"TOM SAWYER"

Imperial Phase

When any writer decides to pen a piece about the best songs over the course of Rush's career, inevitably they'll be faced with a big challenge: which song or songs from *Moving Pictures* should be included, and which will be left out? Universally regarded as Rush's masterpiece, the 1981 album is stacked, front to back, with classic after classic.

The first half alone can easily be considered among the strongest "side ones" in rock history. There's the inimitable and enigmatic "Tom Sawyer," unlikely radio hit and beloved song of air drummers everywhere. Then there's the wistful and multilayered "Red Barchetta," Neil Peart's paean to sports cars, adolescence, and anti-authoritarianism. The nimble, playful, and extremely difficult "YYZ" is Rush's most popular instrumental, popular enough that in 2002, tens of thousands of Brazilian fans famously sang along to a song that had no lyrics. Then there's the endearing, perennial favorite "Limelight," a beautifully catchy song in which Peart lays his heart out, contemplating how difficult it is for a very private artist to live in the public eye.

One can't discount side two, either, which is composed of three songs that dig deeper into Rush's more experimental side. Inspired by the work of author John Dos Passos, "The Camera Eye" is an absorbing, ten-minute suite that finds the band perfecting their new, streamlined brand of progressive rock, first initiated by *Permanent Waves* a year before. "Witch Hunt" is one of the darker tracks in Rush's discography, a commentary on mass hysteria, from religious fanaticism to xenophobia. Closing track "Vital Signs" continues *Permanent Waves*'s exploration of reggae, as well as expanding the use of sequencer.

Multifaceted, rich in musical ideas and lyrical themes, groundbreaking yet extremely approachable—even the complicated parts are wickedly catchy—*Moving Pictures* contains all the elements that make Rush such a special band. It's easy to understand why Peart loved to call *Moving Pictures* the "real" debut album by Rush, because for the first time after years of fine-tuning their sound, they finally reached a place where all three musicians felt at the top of their game. It was a good time for the band: Lee, Lifeson, and Peart were all brimming with new ideas, producer Terry Brown knew how to get the best out of them, and in Le Studio in Morin Heights, Quebec, they found a perfect environment for them to flex their creative muscle, free of outside distraction and pressure.

Better yet, after seven years of steadily growing popularity, thanks to word of mouth among fans, Rush were primed to blow up. Before Lee, Lifeson, and Peart returned to Le Studio with Brown, though, they participated in a fun little side project that would play a massive role in how their eighth album would turn out.

Formed in 1972, Max Webster was a hard-working Toronto band that rose to prominence in the same scene that spawned Rush, and over the years the two bands would become great friends. Max Webster would eventually sign with Rush's label Anthem in 1977, releasing four albums that, buoyed by many tours in support of Rush, would sell well in Canada. Equal parts Cheap Trick, Blue Öyster Cult, and Steely Dan, the band, led by lanky singer/lead guitarist Kim Mitchell, were odd ducks compared to other late-'70s rock acts, but thanks to such endearing singles as "Paradise Skies" and "A Million Vacations," and a gifted lyricist in Toronto poet Pye Dubois, Max Webster was eventually popular enough to headline Canadian hockey arenas by 1980.

So tight was the bond between both bands that on the *Permanent Waves* tour, Peart would warm up by playing along to Max Webster's final three songs of their opening set on his unmiked kit. While arena crowds couldn't hear Neil playing along behind the big black curtain, drummer Gary McCracken sure as hell could. As photographer Rodney Bowes told Martin Popoff, "[Neil would] fuck with Gary. So he'd speed up the beat and he'd double-time it and he would play along. . . . And then afterwards, Neil would have a huge smile and go, 'Hey, good, I only made you fall twice.' Gary says, 'You gotta stop doing that!' He goes, Nope. It's good for you.'"

During the recording of Max Webster's album *Universal Juveniles* in the summer of 1980, Rush approached Mitchell and suggested they record Max Webster's new song "Battle Scar" together, of which they were big fans. After a couple weeks of rehearsal, both bands set up shop in Phase One Studios on July 28, the engineers rigged two 24-track recorders to capture all seven musicians, and the boys hammered out the song live, off the floor, with no headphones. Just amps, two thunderous drummers, and good vibes. Fifteen or sixteen takes later, they had a heavy, imposing beast of a track that would give Max Webster's surging career another big boost.

What the "Battle Scar" collaboration also did was bring together the two lyricists, Peart and Dubois. At one point they started talking about different lyrics they happened to be working on at the moment. Dubois casually mentioned he was tinkering with a poem called "Louie the Lawyer." Neil expressed interest in what he read in Pye's notebook, and before long Dubois gave Peart a couple dozen lines from the poem to see what Neil could come up with in collaboration. The next time they met, Dubois learned that Peart kept a handful of Pye's lines, added a few of his own, and reworked the title. Instead of "Louie the Lawyer," the poem was now called "Tom Sawyer."

From the attention-grabbing opening bars that feature the unforgettable "growl" from Geddy's Oberheim OB-X synthesizer, to the slow yet insistent groove, to the quirky melodies, throttling climax, and hypnotic fade-out, "Tom Sawyer" stands alone in Rush's deep catalog. It's mysterious, brooding yet capable of letting a little light in, and best of all, deceptive. It all sounds simple—minimalist by Rush standards—but for decades Peart called it the most difficult Rush song to play live. "Playing 'Tom Sawyer' properly—or as close as I can get on a given night—requires full mental, technical, and physical commitment, and I can't imagine there would be any way to make that kind of output easier," he told *Drum!* magazine. "And if you ask me, it shouldn't be. If it wasn't hard, it wouldn't be satisfying to get it right!"

As much as Peart dominates the song—it's one of his most thrilling performances on record—the credit for the song's greatness goes to all three members of Rush individually. Each man brings his own distinct and unique touch to the track. Lee is a multi-instrumental wizard, juggling keyboards, synth pedals, and bass guitar with astonishing ease, as well as turning in a riveting vocal performance that further enhances the lyrics' enigmatic nature. Lifeson, meanwhile, moves well beyond straightforward power chords into much more refined, textured guitar work, as well as letting loose a masterful solo that veers into jazz fusion territory. Peart, meanwhile, is a marvel, combining blunt force with smoothness and delicacy, one hand tapping the hi-hat with dexterous speed and the rest of his limbs keeping the pace at a slow, sixty-five-BPM pace. To play fast and slow simultaneously is a massive challenge for any drummer, and Peart took great joy in pursuit of that one elusive, perfect "Tom Sawyer" performance over his long career.

"'Tom Sawyer' is an enjoyable piece of work, mainly based on a funky backbeat rhythm in 4/4, with an instrumental section and rideout in [7/4]," Peart told *Modern Drummer* in 1983. "I'm playing full strength for the whole track, and it took about a day and a half to record. I remember collapsing afterward with raw, red, aching hands and feet. I had been playing the bass drum so hard that my toes were all mashed together and very sore. Physically, this was certainly the most difficult track, and even now it takes as much energy to play properly as my solo."

So excited they were with their newly written track, Rush wasted no time, cutting "Tom Sawyer" the night they loaded in their gear at Le Studio in October 1980. And as soon as that intro kicks in at the beginning of *Moving Pictures*, the line between the prog rock '70s and the more cutting-edge 1980s is apparent. Brown's forty-eight-track production is immaculate—Peart's drums were mixed digitally, a very new thing at the time—the clarity in the mix a far cry from the thicker, more ambiguous tones of the band's early records. It's especially revelatory to hear through a good pair of headphones. Just strap yourself in, crank the volume, and take the ride, just like Chester the Cheetah did on *Family Guy* ("Oh god, there is no fucking drummer better than Neil Peart!"). Though I wouldn't recommend snorting crushed Cheetos.

It's an understated beginning, drums and Oberheim creating a cryptic atmosphere as Geddy coldly narrates Peart's first verse. Tom is immediately established as a strong, resolute individual—there's that theme again—the repeated word "mean" referring not so much to his demeanor as his own self-confidence that he brings to his daily takes, or "battles," if you were.

"TOM SAWYER"

That initial verse is punctuated by one of the song's several defining moments: a series of four-beat ascending riffs that project the power of the song's titular character: duh-duh, duh-DAH. At first it feels as though Alex Lifeson is simply mirroring Geddy's bassline with straightforward power chords, but if you listen closely Alex is doing some surprisingly expressive voicing on guitar. Instead of starting the sequence with E5, D5, A5, C5, he starts with a chiming E major (adding lightness to an otherwise powerful sound) followed by a Dsus2 chord. To this day Lifeson can't explain why he chose that route, but that chord, backed up by Geddy's forceful D note on bass, makes for a beautiful extended chord that sounds just mysterious enough to compel listeners to lean in and wonder what they just heard. With a simple adjustment Lifeson adds so much complexity to an already challenging song, and we're not even 20 seconds in.

Tom is independent, a nonconformist, but don't assume he's full of himself. He may project strength but he's guarded, keeping his emotions to himself. And instead of reacting to anything that happens in his day, he rides them out, just like he rode his raft on the Mississippi River.

The trio returns to that mighty riff sequence, this time with a lot more flavor, Peart's drumming increasing in intensity, Lee providing bass pedal notes that add cinematic flair, like a string section. Then begins a beastly, dramatic riff that first ascends and descends imposingly, as the first of Pye Dubois's verses begins, hinting that if you don't like who Tom chooses to hang out with, you're then

complicit in policing individuals in the way most conformists in society do. Then comes some fun wordplay from Dubois, as he contrasts "mist" and "myth" with "mystery" and "drift," evoking the Mississippi again: its mist in the morning, its mythical status in American lore, its mystery, and its current, on which Tom travels.

The band returns to the simple chord that opens the song, as Dubois elliptically explains that there's a great deal more to love and life than trite, superficial sentiment, and the breadth of it all is just as expansive as Tom's own worldview. In Tom there are no limitations, instead limitless potential, and he approaches life from a completely open and free mind. Neil then chips in a couple lines that illustrate that if a person is gullible and foolish enough, Tom will take full advantage. He doesn't suffer fools lightly.

Right at this moment, Geddy enters with another memorable sequence as the time signature changes from 4/4 to 7/8, a series of synth notes that flit around the arrangement like insects. After a few repetitions Lee switches to bass and Lifeson takes over with a dizzying solo that deftly walks a tightrope as Lee and Peart shift gears from 7/8, to 7/16, to 3/8 time in a manner of seconds. It's something you'd expect from Frank Zappa, a wildly creative solo that adds so much color and detail to the song.

Lifeson's solo leads to the song's most famous moment, the trio building tension more and more until that duh-duh, duh-DAH riff returns and Peart unleashes four monumental drum fills that punctuate the song with a grandiose flourish. Half the fun of seeing Rush play "Tom Sawyer" live was watching so many people mimic those fills when the song reached its summit. It's right up there with John Bonham's crossover triplets in Led Zeppelin's "Dazed and Confused" and Keith Moon's solo in the Who's "Won't Get Fooled Again" as one of the greatest moments in hard rock drumming history.

The song then returns to the creeping refrain, and another crucial verse from Peart. Tom's mind isn't for rent, to anyone. A staunch individualist, Tom can't be bought by either bureaucracy or religion, and at the same time he's cautiously optimistic in his own pragmatic way. Restlessness lies beneath his quixotic nature. And echoing Heraclitus's famous saying, "The only constant in life is change," Tom continues to journey, accepting the fluidity of not only the river but life itself.

Before long, the song hits its outro section, our protagonist continuing on his stoic way, drifting south until he's out of sight. He's his own person, in search of not only his own new experiences but also shared experience with the people he meets. And he'll meet any daily challenge head-on, with pragmatism, inner strength, and joy.

Accentuated perfectly by Hugh Syme's playful, triple-entendre cover photo (deliverymen "moving pictures," the "moving pictures" compelling an elderly couple to cry, a film crew shooting the scene for their own "moving picture"), *Moving Pictures* was an instant success. For the first time in Rush's career, the records and tapes flew off the shelves. Released on February 12, 1981, *Moving Pictures* debuted at number 1 in Canada and peaked at number 3 in both the US and the UK. After years of debt from putting all previous profits into the band's live show, they were all suddenly making money. Almost thirty, the guys were able to pay off mortgages and enjoy holidays abroad with their families. But the machine doesn't stop, and the band embarked on a ninety-five-date North American tour that would have them busy into July.

"Tom Sawyer" remains the iconic moment on a career-defining album and has only grown in stature over the decades. Like "The Spirit of Radio," it immediately became a mandatory setlist inclusion, performed hundreds of times over the next three decades. It is still one of the most-played songs on classic rock radio. Its ubiquity has led to the song appearing in countless movies and television episodes. In *I Love You, Man*, Paul Rudd and Jason Segel bond over their mutual love of Rush, to hilarious effect ("Tom Soyee!"). And who could ever forget the characters from *South Park* rehearsing the song in a special animated video Rush commissioned for their Snakes & Arrows tour?

When you hear a classic rock song repeated so much over the course of your life, its impact can feel muted. However, the mystery and myth of "Tom Sawyer" are still elusive enough to sound as exciting on the one thousandth spin as they do on the first. It's not ubiquitous because an algorithm dictates it; it's ubiquitous because it connected with people in a profound way in 1981 and continues to do so decades later. After all these years, millions are still drawn to the song, to catch the witness, to catch the wit, to catch the spirit, to catch the spit.

Chapter Five Playlist:

"Paradise Skies," Max Webster

"A Million Vacations," Max Webster

"Battle Scar," Max Webster and Rush

"Tom Sawyer," Rush

"Red Barchetta," Rush

"YYZ," Rush

"Limelight," Rush

"The Camera Eye," Rush

"Witch Hunt," Rush

"Vital Signs," Rush

"YYZ" (*Rush in Rio*, 2003), Rush

6

"SUBDIVISIONS"

Perpetual Evolution

Around 1970, Canadian filmmaker Allan King began work on a new documentary that was to depict the generation gap as seen through the eyes of ten youths. "This film grew out of talks with three or four hundred disaffected young people living in the suburban belt surrounding the city of Toronto," the film *Come on Children* prefaces. "A recurring theme emerged: 'Wouldn't it be great if we weren't hassled by parents and police, didn't have to go to prison-like schools, could just get out of this polluted city and into the country and live with a bunch of groovy kids?' Our film was made to explore this notion. We invited five boys and five girls ages thirteen to nineteen to live on a farm, which we provided, for a period of ten weeks, to be filmed, and to see what might emerge for each of them personally."

Among those ten teenagers in this setting that predates MTV's *The Real World* is seventeen-year-old Alex Živojinović, whose girlfriend (and future wife) Charlene had just given birth to their oldest son. He might seem like just another kid from North York, with his long hair, scraggly beard, and thick Toronto accent, but of the ten kids, he's the most mature. His struggles are like those of other teenagers, but he envisions a path in life that he must follow. The difficult part is, however—and anyone who grew up a social misfit can easily relate—that path isn't a conventional one, and as driven as Alex is, it's not easy convincing others that it's worth pursuing.

As a first-generation Canadian whose immigrant parents escaped war in Eastern Europe, it was especially difficult for Alex to tell his mom and dad that he was quitting high school to pursue a career in music. After all, they moved from Yugoslavia to Canada to create a better life and to ensure their children had every opportunity to succeed, so to hear that their son wanted to opt out of the school/college/nine-to-five career trajectory sounded like an affront to them. An exchange late in the film between Alex and his parents encapsulates that difference in philosophy perfectly, and is also an extremely valuable document in the history of Rush, and Canadian music for that matter. So rarely does the public see a future music legend, in their formative years, on camera, with such candor.

"By September we'll be out of debt, just by the money we'll be making," Alex tells Nenad and Melania.

"You know, it's easy to be optimistic when you have security behind you," Nenad interjects, for good reason, "but just think that you'll have nothing to rely on. What are you going to do then?"

"I don't want to make a bunch of money," Alex says. "If I make a lot of money, that's great, but I'm not going to go to university and get a big degree. I don't want to drive around with a big car and everybody goes, 'Hey, there goes Alex, he has a lot of money and wow, he's really set himself up great.' I don't see how I have to go through all the bullshit of high school to learn music. I'm just going to hang around and feel it for a while."

The tension rises as Alex says angrily, "A lot of parents have this great difficulty of listening to their kids, and it is so true."

"You want to say that you know better?" Nenad asks.

"I'm not saying that, Dad. I'm just saying that it would be great if parents sat down and listened to what their kids say, and go, 'That's good that you feel that way, now this is how I feel,' instead of going, 'No that's all wrong, you got to feel like this.' Parents want their kids to turn out like they want them to."

"Kids today want to make us look old," Nenad replies as a withdrawn Alex frowns, disassociating while nervously crumpling a Pepsi can. "And you kids want to be so wise. Experienced. What kind of experience do you have?"

Another father adds, "You know, one of the disappointing things is to see some opportunities available and not being made use of. That's disheartening."

"I have said to you, Alex," Nenad pointedly states, "I want you to be free. To expand. I don't want you to grow up with fear. Or terror. What do you want? That's what I want to know."

Later that night a sullen Alex is idly playing a classical guitar when a roommate asks him what's bothering him. "We talked a lot, but I don't know, we haven't settled anything. Didn't arrive to anything. It's just left there. I feel kind of confused and don't know what to do about it."

"How about if we just let things go," she offers gently to her emotional friend, "and see how they work out?"

"Okay."

That exchange is a perfect encapsulation of postwar white suburban angst, and to anyone who grew up in a similar environment, it cuts very deep. White suburban males comprised a huge chunk of Rush's audience in the 1970s, and although those fans probably didn't see *Come on Children*, there was something in Rush music, lyrics, and personality that made them feel relatable. And you can bet those fans had the exact same teenaged confrontation with their parents as Alex did. Only without a film crew present.

With apologies to Glenn Danzig, Rush were a band of misfits, for misfits. Their music was made for the early *Dungeons & Dragons* crowd, the A/V clubs, the music gear nerds, the sci-fi literature nerds, the outcasts who smoked in the back of the school parking lot. Neil Peart's lyrical subject matter in the 1970s interwove fantasy narratives with individualist philosophy, which felt empowering to anyone who was shunned and bullied in school. Rush in the 1970s was perfect music to escape into. All the stress of another miserable day at school and befuddled parents would disappear as soon as a kid put on a pair of headphones and lost themselves in the intricate musicianship and elaborate storytelling.

Before 1981, Rush had yet to write about that teenaged suburban angst. That would change with "Subdivisions," another landmark track that would not only take Rush's music into new territory but also galvanize the connection between the band and their devoted fans.

During a three-month break from touring in the summer of 1981, Rush were back in Le Studio mixing the live album *Exit . . . Stage Left*, which featured recordings from both the recent *Moving Pictures* tour as well as from the *Permanent Waves* tour the year before. Studio tedium being what it is, the band started jamming for the fun of it. A new Oberheim OB-X synthesizer was too tempting for Geddy Lee to pass up. Inspired by Ultravox's album *Vienna*, a new, keyboard-driven song called "Subdivisions" started to take shape.

Coming off the new direction that *Moving Pictures* signaled, this new song felt like a natural progression. The big difference is that on "Subdivisions," the synths are front and center, driving the song instead of relying on Lifeson's guitar riffs. This, in turn, freed up Lifeson to experiment even more with texture, as well as focus more on rhythm. So while Geddy was leading the way, for the first time Alex and Neil comprised the rhythm section, and this small change in chemistry allowed the two to bond musically more than ever.

Of course, the lyrics were left to Neil, and who knows what possessed him to choose that moment to write about growing up in the suburbs, but what resulted was a vivid, empathetic, heartbreaking song that would become near and dear to many. "How we turn out as adults has a lot to do with the way others saw us in high school," Peart would tell *Classic Rock* magazine decades later. "Consider yourself as a teenager—whether you were treated as a geek, or as a scholar, or a jock, or a good-looking lothario or whatever. However you were treated by others has a lot to do with how you turn out."

Conform, or be cast out. In 1982 especially, it was the honest, brutal truth, and "Subdivisions" spoke to teenagers who were just trying to *survive* school, let alone get passing grades.

It's a dark subject, and that bleakness is reflected in the opening chords of the song, its sense of foreboding echoing the equally murky, minimalist sounds of UK phenoms Joy Division. Repeating twelve times before the rest of the band enters, that looming synth sound is akin to dark clouds that hover over an otherwise idyllic and milquetoast suburban setting. The stage set, Geddy adds more synth melodies that feel brighter yet still melancholic as the musical narrative zooms through those over a green, cleanly laid-out, geometric maze of feeder streets, crescents, and cul-de-sacs. Geddy's voice soon enters, sounding more sensitive than ever before. The more subdued, comfortable timbre exhibited on *Moving Pictures* remains, but there's a lot more compassion in his singing. He clearly relates deeply to Neil's opening lyrics of the geometric orderliness of the suburbs, which, while looking neat and tidy, constrain a lot of the young minds that are growing within its borders.

Since the 1950s, as urban sprawl grew and grew, more and more North American suburbs were built over former farmland, on the very outskirts of the city limits. If you've ever lived on the edge of the 'burbs, that contrast between streetlights and the pitch-black nothingness on the horizon is a deeply uncanny and unsettling sight to witness night after night.

The second half of that first verse echoes the exact scenario that Alex went through with his parents on film, what Geddy and Neil experienced in their own homes, and what any kid reluctant to follow the predesigned path created by twentieth-century capitalism most likely experienced with their own parents. You graduate, you go to college or university, you get married, you work, you have kids, and you work like a dog to provide for your family. To some that's a natural and entirely fair progression in life. For those square pegs who can't fit in society's round holes, though, it's a dead end.

It can be soul-crushing to be a quixotic, imaginative kid with their head in the clouds surrounded by bland suburban development, cookie-cutter architecture, and generic consumer culture. You feel like a prisoner in high school halls. You go to the mall with your friends because there's nothing else to do. You either go to the same old weekend parties in the cool kids' rumpus rooms or you stay at home on Friday night alone, probably listening to Rush. You either find a girlfriend or boyfriend and make out in the back seat of a car, or you stay at home on a Saturday night. Probably listening to Rush. You either do what everyone else is doing, or you spend too much time alone wondering what the hell is wrong with you. Probably while listening to Rush.

Then Geddy sings the key line in the song, the moment where Neil bluntly states what those kids are all feeling but don't have the articulateness to say, and it hits like a punch to the stomach:

escapism for teens in the suburbs provides no real solution for their existential plight. The best the suburbs can offer promising youth is the relentless pursuit of colorless, cookie-cutter heteronormativity, churning out kids and navigating the treacherous terrain of consumerism for the rest of their lives. A good life can be had, but a lot of potential is wasted, too.

Many songs and albums have been written about teen suburban angst, from bands like the Who to Nirvana to Arcade Fire, but few, if any, hit the nail on the head as directly as Neil Peart and Rush do in mere seconds. The sadness in Geddy's voice as he sings the lines is palpable.

Suburban teens can feel so numbed by their environments that venturing into the city center on a weekend night is the only way they can cope with their stultifying existence on the outskirts. And when it's a particularly big city, it can be an awful feeling living an hour away from the nightlife, especially if you don't have access to a car and the public transportation sucks. You might live in the same metro region as that vibrant city, but it can often seem so inaccessible that you might as well be living in China.

Some people are a perfect fit for suburban life, and that's great. Others, though, do put dreams on the back burner in favor of a more stable, predictable life. Or they rush into a career early on and, years, later, suddenly wonder where all the time went, realizing they're in a dead-end job. They might have a spouse and kids, all the trappings of middle-class life, but something feels missing. Before you know it, the cycle repeats, and a person in their forties is sitting at home, mentally lost, and the only escape is to dream of being somewhere else. Or listening to Rush, alone, on a Saturday night.

All of Rush's best songs feature all three members playing to their own specific strengths, and that's certainly the case with "Subdivisions." Geddy, as mentioned, is the driving force, starting with the Oberheim, deftly switching to electric bass, then segueing into mini-Moog synthesizer and bass pedals, and then back to the Oberheim. This song would pave the way for some serious keyboard experimentation on Lee's part for the next decade.

Lifeson's role might sound reduced, but as mentioned earlier he flourishes in his new capacity, playing around the keyboards and interacting more with Peart. The synths are so prominent that producer Terry Brown had a hell of a time trying to make Alex's rhythm guitars as prominent as possible, but many of the rock and metal magazines at the time couldn't—or wouldn't—understand why he wasn't shredding like he used to.

Rolling Stone's resident stick-in-the-mud J. D. Considine meanly wrote, "The band's chief error seems to have been emphasizing synthesizers at the expense of Alex Lifeson's guitar. Because Rush's concept of synthesized sound is so narrow—consisting mainly of the vague whooshing sounds that are the aural equivalent of dry-ice fog—the band tends to sound like it is trapped in wads of lint."

Sounds magazine was ruthless, with Mark Putterford writing, "*Signals* is submerged in a soggy swamp of synthesisers, Moogs and the rest, saturating every song with a needless wall of sound which unmercifully strangles Alex Lifeson's guitar and muffles the usually razor sharp edge to Rush's songs to the extent of making them dull."

It might have sounded at first as though Alex's role was reduced, but "Subdivisions" would not be the great song that it is without his tasteful playing. During the choruses, his arpeggios add plenty of ambience and pathos, while his understated solo later in the song is beautiful as he wrenches as much emotion as he can with each sustained note.

Peart, meanwhile, turns in a drumming clinic for the ages. What he's doing for five minutes sounds simple compared to, say, "The Fountain of Lamneth," but there's a stronger sense of musicality to his drumming here. It's not just bashing away like Keith Moon on speed. There's restraint, texture, knowing when to hold back, and knowing the perfect moment to deliver a devastating fill. If you ever get a chance, track down an isolated drum track from "Subdivisions" online, or better yet, drum cam footage of Neil Peart playing all of "Subdivisions." It's a master at work, refusing to show off yet playing with such authority that it still stops people dead in their tracks.

Completed right before the 1981 tour in support of *Exit . . . Stage Left*, "Subdivisions" was road-tested in Rush's setlists that winter, and once recorded in early 1982, would be the lead-off track on the band's ninth album *Signals*. Despite receiving largely lukewarm reviews, *Signals* was another commercial success, charting at number 1 in Canada, in the top 3 in the UK, and in the top 10 in

America. Better yet, the album had serious legs as the years went by, to the point now where a new generation of music writers, including yours truly, regard it as one of the band's very best albums.

Oddly, the album's biggest single would be the upbeat "New World Man," a song hastily written to even out the sides of the cassette release. It would become a surprise hit in North America, Rush's lone number 1 single in Canada, and their only top 40 hit in America, peaking at 21. As enjoyable as that song is, "Subdivisions" is the song people keep returning to more than four decades later. It was the moment when Rush looked at their audience and showed them just how much they understood where so many of them came from, which is why to this day it's a song that remains near and dear to their fans.

Alex Lifeson revisited that famous clip from *Come on Children* in four decades after the film was released. "You know, the thing is, my parents were right," he laughed. "I thought I knew everything. They came from Yugoslavia, people were getting killed everywhere, my dad was in prison camps. They came to Canada, and their kids are everything. That was I'm sure a great disappointment to them, that I wasn't going to do something that was more professional."

For Alex, his gamble eventually paid off. Like Wayne Gretzky once said, "You miss a hundred percent of the shots you don't take." If a life of conformity isn't for you, all it takes is one brave leap of faith. If you don't take it, as "Subdivisions" vividly states, you might regret that decision for the rest of your life.

Chapter Six Playlist:

"Astradyne," Ultravox

"Vienna," Ultravox

"Atmosphere," Joy Division

"Love Will Tear Us Apart," Joy Division

"Ceremony," New Order

"A Forest," The Cure

"Subdivisions," Rush

"New World Man," Rush

"Chemistry," Rush

"The Weapon," Rush

"Losing It," Rush

7

"BETWEEN THE WHEELS"

A Different Kind of Heavy

By 1983, a new generation of hard rock and heavy metal musicians was starting to overtake their 1970s progenitors, cherry-picking traits from their favorite bands and creating unique, groundbreaking new musical hybrids in the process. Many of those young artists, especially in America and Canada, were heavily influenced by Rush's 1970s work, the *2112* album especially. Chief among those bands was Metallica, whose bassist Cliff Burton and guitarist Kirk Hammett were profoundly inspired by the musical and conceptual ideas of *2112*, and in 1983 and 1984 quickly became the standard-bearers for heavy metal by embracing that progressive side of Rush with rawer, more underground influences such as Motörhead and Venom.

The boys in Rush were very much aware of this new wave of young bucks taking rock and metal music into more aggressive, more extreme new territory, and they themselves were wowed by what they heard and saw. Geddy Lee would see Metallica live for the first time in Toronto in 1985 and leave the venue floored by the band's mix of intensity, dexterity, and melody. Fully aware of their connection to the '80s metal movement, Rush would embrace it by having many young metal bands open for them during that decade, thereby attracting a younger crowd to their own shows as well.

What's so interesting about this period in Rush's history is that while heavy metal was rapidly evolving, getting more aggressive seemingly by the month, Rush's own sound was retreating more and more from the heavier sounds of *2112* and *Hemispheres*. Each record after *Hemispheres* was one step further away from the over-driven, distorted riffs and solos of the 1970s. They refused to be rock dinosaurs, and *Permanent Waves*, *Moving Pictures*, and *Signals* saw Rush creating their own unique niche in rock music by constantly looking ahead instead of behind.

Musical experimentation in the early 1980s was driven heavily by technology, and Geddy Lee was all over it at that time, enthralled by every new advancement in synthesizers, digital sequencers, and electronic percussion that came down the pike. It got to the point where by 1984 his side of the stage (stage left) would be dominated by an ever-expanding bank of keyboards: a PPG Wave 2.2, a Roland JP-8 and a TR 808, the very fashionable Oberheim OBX-A, a DSX digital sequencer, as well as his trusty Moog Taurus pedals and Minimoog. At a time when synthesizers were frowned upon by the heavy metal crowd, all that digital technology would play a huge role in what would arguably become Rush's heaviest record, 1984's *Grace Under Pressure*.

Sonically heavy (yes, even with lots of synths), thematically heavy, and recorded during a bitterly cold winter under circumstances that would become increasingly arduous the more the painfully slow process dragged on, *Grace Under Pressure* is an enigmatic outlier in the Rush discography. Its lyrics delve deep into paranoia, sadness, intergenerational trauma, and bleakness, the bright-sounding keyboards and sequencers offset by an ominous, almost murky lower end. Geddy's synth melodies slice and slash, Alex's solos are tinged with sorrow, and when Neil isn't hitting his drums with incredible force, he's creating palpable tension with Stewart Copeland–inspired texture. Adding to that heavy mood was the sheer amount of time the band put into the recording, which commenced at the beginning of November 1983 and ended on March 12, 1984, working every day save for a ten-day break over Christmas. The band was so stressed over the whole process that Lee would admit years later that the sessions nearly destroyed his marriage.

Writing and rehearsal for the follow-up to *Signals* went smoothly. The band set up shop just north of Toronto in Barrie, Ontario, in August 1983. "Kid Gloves," "Afterimage," "Red Sector A," and "The Body Electric" were among the new songs the threesome briskly put together, but the best of the lot, "Between the Wheels," was the first song written, completed in a mere twenty minutes. So confident was the band in the new material that a month later, during a five-night stand in New York City at Radio City Music Hall, "Red Sector A," "The Body Electric," and "Kid Gloves" debuted.

Being huge fans of new British music, Rush had enlisted the services of producer Steve Lillywhite, their first record without longtime collaborator Terry Brown at the helm. By 1983 Lillywhite was very much in demand, having produced such landmark albums as U2's *Boy*, *October*, and *War*; Peter Gabriel's classic third solo album; Big Country's hit *The Crossing*; and The Psychedelic Furs' *Talk Talk Talk*. Nabbing Lillywhite at this moment in time was a real coup, but much to the band's dismay he bowed out two weeks before sessions were scheduled to begin, jumping ship to work with Simple Minds instead on their 1984 album *Sparkle in the Rain*.

Suddenly faced with a serious dilemma, Rush quickly scrambled to see who was available to produce the album. Trevor Horn, who masterminded two 1983 classics in Yes's career-saving *90125* and Frankie Goes to Hollywood's epochal single "Relax," was at the top of the list, as was Yes bassist Chris Squire and the Fixx's producer Rupert Hine, but with the band already well into preproduction on their own, they decided to go with Peter Henderson, who was best known for having produced Supertramp's bestseller *Breakfast in America*.

As everyone settled in at Le Studio for the winter, the band quickly found out that Henderson, while a gifted engineer, didn't take charge enough to the guys' liking, leaving Geddy, Alex, and Neil to agonize over minutiae that Terry Brown would have gladly handled. Lee would describe the ordeal with Henderson to the *Los Angeles Times* in 1986: "We didn't achieve what we started out to.

What happened is that we got so caught up in making it we weren't looking at it objectively enough. . . . The whole thing was convoluted and confused. It could have been done a whole lot better. We thought we had solved the problem but we hadn't."

What resulted was the aptly titled *Grace Under Pressure*, an album that cleverly juxtaposed bright, modern arrangements with the bleakest lyrics of Rush's career. A reflection of Cold War anxiety, its tension is still palpable today. Adding to the album's overall angst was the approaching year 1984, which had media relentlessly pondering just how Orwellian the Western world had become. (Consequently, sales of the novel *1984* went through the roof around this time.) Additionally, the word "red" appears often throughout the album: the DEFCON-referencing "red alert," the Communist "red book" and subsequent "red scare," the "red sector" of a concentration camp, "seeing red" (anger), "rocket's red glare" (jingoistic propaganda), and on and on.

Opening track and lead single "Distant Early Warning" sets the tone immediately, its bright melodies backed by Peart's taut, nervous drumming and, of course, led by his anguished lyrics. Referencing the series of radar stations in the Arctic operated by the United States, Canada, Greenland, and Iceland at the height of the Cold War, Peart expresses helplessness and compassion ("What am I to do? You sometimes drive me crazy, but I worry about you"). Geddy's cries of "Absolom! Absolom!" at the end reference the biblical phrase, "Would God I had died for thee," a cry of self-sacrificing love.

Part Blue Öyster Cult, part Police, all Rush, "Afterimage" is a sorrowful tribute to the band's friend Robbie Whelan, a Le Studio tape operator who had died in a car accident the previous year. The pulsating, sequencer-driven "Red Sector A" sees Peart writing from the point of view of a World War II concentration camp prisoner, a subject near and dear to Geddy Lee, whose parents survived that very ordeal. Anxiety permeates the paranoid "The Enemy Within" as its narrator battles with their inner demons, determined to not let fear derail them from their goals, but as we all know, it's never an easy fight.

Inspired by Ray Bradbury's short story "I Sing the Body Electric!"—which in turn gets its title from Walt Whitman—the equally tense "The Body Electric" explores the idea of possible consciousness and free will within artificial intelligence, or as Peart once described, "'2112' for robots." By far the most optimistic moment on the album, the bright "Kid Gloves" establishes a snappy little 5/4 groove as Peart writes about how important self-compassion is when it comes to making difficult decisions in life ("Handle with kid gloves / Then you learn the lessons / Taught in school won't be enough"). Meanwhile, "Red Lenses" veers right into Adrian Belew–era King Crimson territory, loaded with atonal riffs, electronic percussion, jazzy grooves, and some spoken-sung vocals by Geddy that totally mimic Belew's singing style on King Crimson's classic 1981 *Discipline* album. Continuing with the "red" theme, King Crimson's 1973 album *Red* is revered by many Rush fans, and 1981's *Discipline* boasts vivid, red cover art.

The first seven tracks on *Grace Under Pressure* steadily build toward a somber denouement on "Between the Wheels," one of the subtler songs in Rush's discography. A side two deep cut, "Between the Wheels" was never a single, nor did it receive a lot of attention when the record came out. Listeners' ears immediately went to more urgent, catchier tracks like "Distant Early Warning," "Afterimage," and "Red Sector A," and only the die-hard fans would flip the record over to the stranger, more experimental side two. The band was kind of the same way, too, and only rediscovered the magic and power of "Between the Wheels" when they decided to dust it off and bring it back to the setlist nearly twenty years later.

It feels ironic how such a challenging, thematically deep song was the first and easiest song Rush wrote for *Grace Under Pressure*, but in retrospect the gloomy, doomy musical tone of the composition set the stage for the difficult recording process that would follow. It's a dark, very heavy song, something listeners hear immediately with Geddy's unsettling, metronomic synth line evoking the *diabolus in musica*, the tritone, masterfully accentuated by Alex's roaring, Sabbath-esque power chords. Structurally it's not different from what's heard on *Signals*, but the production by Henderson and the band is much beefier, more analog in tone. It feels simultaneously warm and frigid, like sun on permafrost, as Lifeson plays a mournful melody while the song slowly trudges toward the first verse.

Peart sets up the mise-en-scène quickly, depicting life in the early 1980s: baby boomers in North America sought escapism from the nuclear threat by watching television, their children caught in a surreal period where the Vietnam War was a memory, but the world didn't exactly feel peaceful either.

The song quickly shifts to a sprightly double-time tempo, but any optimism is quickly dashed by Peart's brutal imagery. Time has a way of catching up to a person, and before they know it, the end is staring them in the face, and all they can do is stand, stunned like a rodent caught in the headlights of a fast-approaching vehicle. You're frozen in time, the split second between life and death hanging in the air, but those vehicle wheels, the wheels of time, if you will, don't care. If you're not along for the ride, time has no problem continuing without you. It's a horrifying thing to consider, but also more than enough motivation to live every moment like it's the last.

The wheel, one of the most epochal inventions in the history of humankind, can harm as much as it can help. It's crucial for transportation, but as a tool it can crush, grind, slice. The economy can tank at any given moment, and anyone can go from being on the cusp of intellectual or spiritual enlightenment to just another lifeless piece of flesh on the ground. "Bowl of dust" also references the Great Depression of the 1930s, when lack of crop rotation, drought, and windstorms transformed the Great Plains into what was commonly referred to as the "Dust Bowl." The melody gently shifts to almost hopeful, offering a tiniest glimmer of light, before quickly fizzling out, evoking not only the Lost Generation of the 1920s but also the Beat Generation of the postwar '50s and the angst-ridden Generation X of the 1990s. It all seems so hopelessly cyclical.

Peart juxtaposes blind American patriotism with the harsh reality of tough economic times by evoking both "The Star-Spangled Banner" and the 1930s Depression-era song "Brother, Can You Spare a Dime?" We're all another world war away from some truly dystopian times, and the young generation of 1984—what would come to be known as Generation X—would become another disillusioned demographic just like the Lost Generation of the 1920s and the post–World War II Beat Generation.

The passage of time is evoked by another wheel analogy: this time, the wheel of the film reel, which mechanically whips image after image through the projector, never stopping, always relentlessly moving forward until the film runs out.

The pace of modern life was already manic enough in 1984. Today it's even worse, and Peart's final verse hits particularly hard decades after it was originally written. The real world is overwhelming: we work to survive; rent, mortgages, and inflation are out of control; we barely have enough time on any given day; the news is constantly depressing and traumatic; popular culture is getting shallower and triter by the year; the idea of "easy street" or the American dream is nothing but a myth, a lie used to compel individuals to sacrifice their well-being to boost the economy and "look out for number one." In the end, it often feels like the safest we can feel is to lock ourselves in the bedroom, get under the covers, and stay there until things on the outside get better. Coming at the end of Rush's darkest album, it's one hell of a buzzkill, a sobering dose of reality.

It doesn't get much heavier than that.

Chapter Seven Playlist:

"The Four Horsemen," Metallica

"Intruder," Peter Gabriel

"Pretty in Pink," The Psychedelic Furs

"Relax," Frankie Goes to Hollywood

"Are We Ourselves?," The Fixx

"Breakfast in America," Supertramp

"Distant Early Warning," Rush

"Elephant Talk," King Crimson

"Red Lenses," Rush

"Red Sector A," Rush

"Between the Wheels," Rush

8

"TIME STAND STILL"

Prog Goes Pop

Just as Rush had done at the dawn of the 1980s, many other progressive rock bands and musicians were starting to shift with the times as well. Like Rush, some streamlined their sound just for a change of pace, to break from the Sisyphean task of having to top the previous complicated prog rock opus by writing an even more complicated prog rock opus. Others were inspired by the huge technological advancements happening at the time; as the previous chapter mentioned, digital technology was growing by leaps and bounds. Others felt like cultural dinosaurs, rendered irrelevant by younger, more exciting bands like the Clash, Talking Heads, the Police, Devo, and many more. And some clearly saw dollar signs as they witnessed such bands as Boston and Journey top charts and sell out arenas with their hook-oriented, stadium-ready hard rock. A prog band could easily do that, with just the right ingredients.

The exact moment "when prog went pop" is a little hazy, but several different events happened that triggered the movement. After leaving Genesis in 1975, Peter Gabriel kicked off his solo career in 1977 with the astounding "Solsbury Hill"; lyrically poetic yet far more musically direct than anything he'd done with Genesis, it was a top 20 single in the UK and would become an enduring classic as the decades went by. In early 1980 Pink Floyd scored their only US number 1 single with arguably the most nihilistic chart-topper in history, the disco-tinged "Another Brick in the Wall (Part 2)." Gabriel's former bandmates didn't top the charts with 1980's "Turn It on Again," but it set Genesis off in a direction that would see them dominate the pop charts well into the 1980s. The Moody Blues took a page from ELO's art pop book on the platinum *Long Distance Voyager* album. And going back to Genesis, drummer Phil Collins became the unlikeliest male artist to dominate the 1980s, kicking off a wildly successful solo career with 1981's groundbreaking "In the Air Tonight," whose drum sound would set the template for pop and rock music for the rest of the decade. In fact, Collins, Genesis, and Gabriel would become such powerful pop entities on their own that Genesis's *Invisible Touch* album would hit number 1 in America in May 1986, only to be toppled by Gabriel's album *So* in June.

Then there was Asia, who, for one hot moment, became one of the biggest rock bands in the world, whose residuals would make life comfy for four progressive rock veterans. Formed by Yes guitarist Steve Howe, former King Crimson bassist and singer John Wetton, former Yes keyboardist Geoff Downes, and drummer Carl Palmer (of Emerson, Lake & Palmer), Asia's 1982 debut album is almost clinical in the way it interweaves progressive rock and arena rock. The crystalline production, with its layers of roaring guitars and the sublime, radio-friendly hooks made the album a massive hit, especially in North America, thanks to the top five single "Heat of the Moment."

One year later, Yes, whose four-side, four-song *Tales from Topographic Oceans* epitomized prog excess in 1975, scored an unfathomable number 1 single in the form of the flashy, forward-looking "Owner of a Lonely Heart" and found themselves pop music darlings. Trevor Horn's innovative production—the song one of the first examples of a sample being used as a breakbeat—made "Owner of a Lonely Heart" one of the most cutting-edge rock songs of that year, practically bringing Yes back from the dead and extending the band's career into the 1980s and beyond.

Although Rush didn't exactly achieve success on the singles charts like their British peers, their similarly streamlined sound, adjusted to reflect what was happening around them—musical growth, digital technology, stylistic changes in rock music—kept '80s rock fans engaged enough to ensure consistent album sales. In Canada, Rush benefited immensely from the country's rigid Canadian Content (CanCon) rules, especially during the 1980s, when music videos were booming.

Instituted in 1971, CanCon was a strategy developed by the Canadian Radio-television and Telecommunications Commission (CRTC) not only to ensure Canadian artists and content got airplay (extremely important for Canadian arts and culture, given that the United States is such a pop culture behemoth) but also to develop a strong, vibrant arts culture in the future. Radio was required to devote 30 percent of its content to Canadian artists, which in turn played a huge role in building the infrastructure that a healthy recording industry needed. The airplay, coupled with heavy touring across the huge expanse that is Canada, benefited Rush immensely, and by the beginning of the '80s they consistently put out top 40 singles in their home country.

It was the advance of the music video in the early 1980s, however, that Canada's percolating star system started to realize its potential, and the timing of Rush's more mainstream-friendly sound could not have been more perfect. Rush was the biggest Canadian rock band at the time that benefited most from guaranteed Canadian airplay on music video channels and programs. When Canada's answer to MTV, the irreverent, groundbreaking MuchMusic, launched on August 31, 1984, their first video they played was Rush's new single "The Enemy Within." The band would go on to have a good relationship with the network from then on, even having MuchMusic shoot Rush's hometown concert on September 21, 1984, which was broadcast in 1985 and released on VHS and Betamax in March 1986.

Power Windows was released on October 11, 1985, recorded over the spring and summer under conditions that were a lot less stressful for the band. Partnering with producer Peter Collins (who had previously produced albums by Musical Youth, Nik Kershaw, and Tygers of Pan Tang) Rush had found the right collaborator to help pull off the sound they wanted for album number eleven. Intended as a combination of the best aspects of *Signals* and *Grace Under Pressure*, *Power Windows* is high gloss to the point of feeling as cold as chrome.

Geddy Lee's keyboards and synthesizers dominate the record, as do his strong vocal melodies, but Alex Lifeson's guitars are a lot more prominent, which lends the sound the right amount of bite. Keyboardist Andy Richards, best known for playing a huge role on two chart-toppers—Frankie Goes to Hollywood's "Relax" and George Michael's "Careless Whisper"—was brought on to add additional synth programming, and his flashy, dynamic flourishes are all over such tracks as "The Big Money" and "Territories." Adding to the unique sound of the album is Geddy's new favorite bass guitar, a long-scale Wal Custom. Unlike his traditional favorites, the Rickenbacker and the Fender Jazz, the Wal had more of a "popping" sound, which allowed Geddy to add more funk and jazz fusion elements into his bass playing. And he shreds all over the album, his lithe, nimble basslines creating clever countermelodies underneath the vocals, keyboards, and guitars.

Neil Peart's lyrics on *Power Windows* are all ruminations on the theme of power, ranging from corporate power, nationalist power, and scientific power to feeling either powerless, physically powerful, or as he addresses on the gorgeous "Mystic Rhythms" (one of Rush's most underrated songs), spiritual power. It all sounds so serious to the point where casual listeners would wonder if these guys are actually having fun, but the bright, accessible arrangements—which sounded contemporary in 1985—and strong melodies offset the rather pensive lyrical tone, and the record-buying public agreed, catapulting the album to the top 10 in the US, Canada, and the UK. The album would grow on the band too; during the Clockwork Angels tour in 2012 and 2013, five *Power Windows* songs were included in the setlist.

As good as *Power Windows* is—and it's damn good—the defining moment from Rush's Great Pop Experiment era comes from one of their weakest albums. 1987's *Hold Your Fire* isn't a catastrophically bad record—in fact, Peter Collins's production is sublime, as pristine as any other record that came out that year—but it's the first time Rush strayed a little too far from what made their previous 1980s music so exceptional. Too many songs flirted with sounding generic, awash in lavish synthesizer arrangements. Alex's guitars were treated almost as an afterthought, and tracks like "Mission" and "Lock and Key" felt far too light, sorely lacking the muscle that gave previous albums just the right enough sense of dynamics. And the less said about the ham-fisted "Tai Shan," the better.

"Time Stand Still," on the other hand, feels like a miracle in comparison, the moment where all the right moments coalesce into five transcendent minutes of music. Built around a gentle little chiming guitar riff by Lifeson, it's a surprisingly brisk song that finds Peart in a particularly self-reflective mood. "All through the '70s our lives were flying by; we spent so much time on the road that it became like a dark tunnel," he told the *Boston Globe* in 1987. "You start to think about the people you're neglecting, friends and family. So the song is about stopping to enjoy that; with a warning against too much looking back. Instead of getting nostalgic about the past, it's more a plea for the present."

Just as Genesis had pulled off on their massive global hit "Invisible Touch" a year before, Rush cleverly decorates a progressive rock song (Geddy's perky bassline, again on his beloved Wal, is a masterclass in balancing rhythm and melody) with enough pop window dressing to make it palatable for the masses. Lifeson's chiming, faux-acoustic notes kick off "Time Stand Still," with Peart adding his trademark tom-tom flourishes before settling into a tight little backbeat with Geddy, who quickly enters with the first verse. Peart's lyrics begin as he catches himself looking back on his life during a moment of pause during his travels, yet also feeling as though his constant state of movement is preventing him from experiencing the simple pleasures, like simple conversation with a pal. He expresses vulnerability and wishes he could live in the moment more, to embrace the present rather than live in the past.

It's at this moment where we hear the voice of Aimee Mann appear, the first (and only) time a guest vocalist appears on a Rush song. Peart had the idea of bringing in a female voice to punctuate the chorus, and the band reached out to Cyndi Lauper and Chrissie Hynde, but neither artist was available. Mann, however, was suggested, and the idea made a lot of sense. Rush were already great admirers of Mann's band 'Til Tuesday (especially the 1986 track "What About Love") and she agreed to contribute vocals to "Time Stand Still." It turned out to be a perfect fit, as her timbre is a perfect match for Geddy's voice, and the two make a formidable duo during the ethereal chorus.

The song then explodes into its most exuberant hook, as Peart longs to freeze every present moment so he can savor the experience, because once it's done, it's done, disappearing faster than water through fingers.

Neil's second verse sees him trying desperately to change the way he perceives the world around him, but past traumas are always exposed the moment he opens himself up (his wordplay of "wounds" and "unwound" is particularly clever). If he could stop the world just so he could take a calm, cleansing breath in the midst of all the chaos around him, he would.

Interestingly, there's no guitar solo by Lifeson. Instead, the song glides gracefully at a 7/8 pace, accentuated by Mann's gorgeous vocalizing, building to a majestic crescendo that comfortably settles into the chorus again. This time, Peart alters his post-chorus lines, adding more urgency to his message, complete with a little nod to William Blake's *Songs of Innocence and Experience* at the end.

The older you get, the faster time seems to go by, and it's hard not to panic about not enjoying the present more than you already have. For a band like Rush, who not for a second ever wanted to replicate past records or lean on a tried-and-true formula, "Time Stand Still" could also be a statement by the band about how they approach their art. Instead of relying on the past, they'd rather keep learning, keep evolving, and make music that reflects where they are now.

The video for "Time Stand Still," directed by Academy Award–winning filmmaker Zbigniew Rybczyński, was cutting-edge at the time, but to say it hasn't aged gracefully is an understatement. Rybczyński's editor Glenn Lazzaro wrote hilariously about the video shoot, "I suggested that we shoot them live on the stage, but Zbig wanted everyone to 'float' around it. He also insisted that everything had to happen 'live.' Each new layer would be placed on top of the preceding layer without making protection copies or 'laying off' a copy, as we used to say. . . . Zbig would give some vague direction to Rush; I would set up the effects, play the audio track and press record, causing multiple one-inch tape machines to roll up on the third floor. For three days in a row."

Geddy would tell *Rolling Stone* in 2013, "My daughter saw this video for the first time because they featured some of it in [the Rush documentary *Beyond the Lighted Stage*]. She just thought it was hilarious that we were flying through the air. It's such a strange video. It was just a bizarre day. . . . This is my hair at its worst. It's a bad 'do. The funny thing is just watching this giant drum kit flying through the air. It's one thing to see humans. They have a form. But here's this whole drum kit floating through space. Who says we don't have a sense of humor?"

Sadly, "Time Stand Still" didn't light up the charts the same way Genesis's "Invisible Touch" did, although it did receive heavy airplay in Canada. In fact, the response to *Hold Your Fire* was muted, sales stalling not long after its release. Today, it remains the only

Rush album, along with *Caress of Steel*, to not be certified platinum in America.

Rush's tour in support of *Hold Your Fire* still went well, yielding the live album and concert film *A Show of Hands* in early 1989. Eager to right the wrongs they felt were made on the previous album, Rush attempted a reset, bringing in producer Rupert Hine, who had not only worked with such prog and prog-adjacent acts as Camel and Saga but also on Tina Turner's landmark *Private Dancer*. Released in 1989, Presto has moments where Rush rediscover their magic, especially on opening track "Show Don't Tell," which blends a nifty prog groove with grandiose pop rock. "Chain Lightning" and "War Paint" show similar muscle, while the elegiac ballad "The Pass" is one of the most genuinely moving songs the band ever recorded. Sadly, the rest of the album can't sustain the momentum, as songs like "Superconductor," "Hand Over Fist," and "Available Light" fall incredibly flat.

1991's *Roll the Bones* fared a lot better commercially. The band sounds more focused, and you can hear that urgency on "Dream-line," which would become a surprise rock radio hit in America and go on to be a concert staple for the next two decades. The title track, contentious as it would be among fans, would go on to be an enduring favorite of the band's. The "rap" section during the break-down is so unapologetically goofy that it's kind of charming. When a pitch-shifted Geddy kicks in with Peart's verses, it sounds like a nerdy dad deliberately embarrassing his kid in front of their friends with the most deliberately cringey rap ever, including a declaration that he's going to kick some, erm, gluteus max.

When the band begins again and MC Geddy (Lil Ged?) snarls "get bizz-ay!" you can picture the guys killing themselves laughing in the studio, perhaps under the influence of jazz cigarettes and good wine. Only Rush could get away with an idea that corny and somehow make it work. *Roll the Bones* sold well, no mean feat considering the rock landscape was about to experience a seismic shift at the end of 1991 thanks to Kurt Cobain and Nirvana. But that shift in musical taste, on the part of audiences, record companies, and musicians, would compel Rush to give pause and wonder if it was time to recalibrate again. For all intents and purposes, Rush's Great Pop Experiment was over.

Chapter Eight Playlist:

"Turn It on Again," Genesis
"In the Air Tonight," Phil Collins
"Heat of the Moment," Asia
"Owner of a Lonely Heart," Yes
"The Big Money," Rush
"Mystic Rhythms," Rush

"Invisible Touch," Genesis

"What About Love," 'Til Tuesday

"Time Stand Still," Rush

"The Pass," Rush

"Roll the Bones," Rush

9

"ANIMATE"

Power Trio

When Nirvana's epochal album *Nevermind* supplanted Michael Jackson's *Dangerous* at number 1 in America the week of January 11, 1992, record industry attitudes toward what constituted fashionable rock music turned immediately. Suddenly "grit" was in, "flash" was out. The "slowed-down punk" sound of grunge was more commercially appealing than ostentatious shredding. Mainstream hard rock artists who enjoyed strong sales in 1991—Skid Row, Warrant, Alice Cooper—were deemed passé, and only the biggest hard rock bands at the time (Metallica, Aerosmith, and Guns N' Roses) came out unscathed. Consequently, bands who relied on one specific rock formula in the 1980s started to scramble, tuning down their guitars, slowing down the tempos, in a desperate attempt to stay relevant. From Mötley Crüe to Exodus, '80s bands were now chasing trends instead of sticking to their strengths. Hell, even thrash innovators Megadeth started wearing plaid flannel onstage.

Always keenly aware of how rock music was progressing, Rush was aware of the seismic shift in mainstream rock music. They loved bands like Soundgarden and Pearl Jam and were wowed by the wild creativity of Primus, who opened for Rush on the *Roll the Bones* tour. Hearing the heaviness of Cream and Zeppelin and Black Sabbath creep back into mainstream rock was an especially exciting development for Alex Lifeson, who after dutifully scaling back on his riff-oriented playing style for the past decade and change was ready to step to the forefront once again. He didn't want to be a supporting player anymore, and his itch to get back to Rush's power trio basics created friction when the band started writing their fifteenth album.

"There were certainly a lot more fights during these sessions," Geddy Lee told *Raw* magazine in 1993. "Almost every Monday morning Alex and I would have a full-blown, in-your-face argument. . . . You could see it coming on the last tour.

"Alex is very reactionary. He must have said 10,000 times that he didn't want any keyboards on the album, so when I brought my keyboards into the studio there was an immediate atmosphere. He kept looking at them like they were really threatening. . . . It was a very volatile situation."

Feeling that their recent work with Rupert Hine had softened and thinned out their sound too much, Rush decided to reunite with Peter Collins, who after the commercial disappointment of *Hold Your Fire* in 1987 bounced back, producing an impressive string of strong-selling albums over the next five years by such artists as Queensrÿche, Gary Moore, Alice Cooper, and Suicidal Tendencies. In order to ensure the new album retained a stronger, more muscular sound than *Roll the Bones*, Collins brought in a brash young engineer from South Africa named Kevin "Caveman" Shirley, and while his methods would excite Geddy and Alex, they would quickly become a huge pain in Neil Peart's backside.

Anyone familiar with Shirley's style—especially on his extensive work with Iron Maiden since 2000—knows that the man loves a big wall of sound. He lives for the experience of a band playing live, and all his recordings try to capture that feel as accurately as possible, even if it means muddying up the tracks a bit. He wants his bands to sound like one organism on record, not an assemblage of finely honed instrumental parts. For a guy like Neil Peart, who loved to hear every little beat of percussion on record, that didn't seem like much fun at all.

Alex took a lot of convincing, but he slowly started to catch on to the method behind Shirley's madness. Shirley insisted Alex go back to his Les Paul and Telecaster—setting aside his expensive PRS guitars, which Shirley would say looked more like coffee tables than guitars—and record his guitar parts directly in front of the amps to feel the resonance of the riffs he played; by forcing Lifeson to pay attention to the hum and sustain of the guitar, it allowed him to connect more innately with the music, to capture that intangible feel that so many guitarists chase. Geddy, meanwhile, agreed to ditch the Wal bass he'd been using since 1985, went back to the Fender Jazz with heavier strings, and plugged into a rickety old Ampeg amplifier that Shirley had found. The hugely overdriven buzz and crunch of that unpredictable amp captured the heaviness of Geddy's basslines like they hadn't heard since *Moving Pictures*, so Mr. Lee was all in.

Additionally, Shirley was never one to worry about instruments bleeding into one another; in fact, he encouraged it, believing that having the drums bleed into the guitar pickup enhanced the overall sound of the guitar. For Rush, who had grown to love the minutiae of recording, this was a radical change. Peart loved nuance, he loved subtlety. He didn't want John Bonham–style thunder. Nevertheless, Shirley insisted on recording Peart's drums with minimal microphones rather than having a mic on every single drum. Meanwhile, Collins, also concerned with groove and feel more than accuracy, would keep cajoling Neil to relax and be "in the pocket" more. With all three members of Rush trying to wrap their heads around a passive-aggressive producer and a very outspoken engineer, it made for a strange dynamic at Le Studio in the summer of 1993.

"Geddy was a lot of fun, very easygoing, very straightforward to work with," Shirley would tell Martin Popoff. "He was concerned with detail, the minutiae, whereas Alex was very much concerned about where he was in the big picture. Alex was more abrasive in the studio—it was always more of a threat to him; the process was more difficult for him. And Neil, we never saw Neil. He came in and drummed and went back to his little room—and smoked wads of weed."

When all was said and done, *Counterparts* was released on October 19, 1993. The churning "Stick It Out" was the ideal choice for the first single, far and away the heaviest song Rush had recorded in many years, and it fit very well with the direction rock radio had taken in the previous year or two, debuting at number 1 on Billboard's Album (later renamed Mainstream) Rock Tracks chart. The fans loved what they heard, and *Counterparts* peaked at number 2 on the Billboard Album Chart, number 6 in Canada, and 14 in the UK.

Typical of 1990s rock music, an era when the seventy-nine-minute CD format compelled bands and labels to cram as much music onto a disc as possible, *Counterparts* flirts with bloat at a hefty fifty-four minutes, but it's hard to blame the band for being excited to showcase their new change in direction. It remains a very strong title in Rush's discography, bolstered by such standouts as the hard-driving "Cut to the Chase," the immensely fun instrumental "Leave That Thing Alone," and the poignant "Nobody's Hero." The rawness of the production offsets the intricate melodies surprisingly well, making for a much cleaner sound than a lot of rock records that came out in 1993. Peart is indeed in the pocket nicely, Geddy's in outstanding vocal form, and Alex sounds liberated after spending far too long in the background. And although there are keyboards, they're only added as backing enhancement, never placed in the foreground.

As strong as *Counterparts* is overall, it peaks on the first track. Never released as a single, the propulsive yet highly contemplative

"Animate" is now considered a minor classic, a song the band always loved to play, right until their final show in 2015. It's a song that seems simple on the surface but is layered with some of Neil's thematically complex and deepest lyrics to date.

Peart sets the tone immediately, his count of, "One, two, three, four, one, two," announces that the Rush of 1993 intends to get back to the organic, rock side of their sound. The drum pattern that Neil launches into is especially interesting: it sounds forceful, but relaxed as well, evidence that Collins's insistence that the drums stay more "in the pocket" worked extremely well in the end. And this isn't your usual Neil Peart drumbeat, either. It's steady, hypnotic, never changing until a quick instrumental break at the 3:20 mark where Neil shifts into more tribal-themed tom-tom patterns. That central drumbeat, it turns out, was highly influenced by the trendy "shoegaze" sound coming out of the UK, with Neil specifically citing the bands Lush and Curve as big inspirations for his approach on "Animate."

Led by My Bloody Valentine, whose leader Kevin Shields redefined "guitar rock" on 1991's groundbreaking *Loveless*, what started as an indie rock subscene had blown up by 1992 as audiences were drawn to those massive layers of effects-laden guitars, barely discernable lead vocals—often female—and hypnotic drum grooves that themselves were lifted straight out of the Beatles' "Tomorrow Never Knows." Peart does an outstanding job replicating that beat, infusing it with his distinctive power.

After a couple bars, Geddy enters with a thrumming, six-teenth-beat bassline that is clearly pushing that ancient Ampeg to the limit, while Alex adds melody and texture to the central riff melody, which is subtly enhanced by the slightest hint of synthe-sizer. Geddy kicks into Peart's first verse, which feels a lot more abstract than longtime fans are used to from this storyteller.

Writing his essay for Rush's tour book in 1993, Peart explains that "Animate" is "about one man addressing his anima—his fem-inine side, as defined by Carl Jung. Within that duality, what 'a man must learn to gently dominate' is himself, his own 'submis-sive trait,' while also learning to 'gently dominate' the animus—the male thing—and the other hormone driven 'A-words' like aggres-sion and ambition. We dominate by not submitting, whether to brute instinct, violent rage, or ruthless greed."

That notion plays right into the second verse, which shifts into a more biting, nimble rhythm riff by Alex and Geddy as Peart's lyrics get to the crux of his idea for the song. In researching his idea for a song that explored the notion of duality, Peart found him-self immersed in the work of Jung and Camille Paglia, explaining to radio host Steve Warden in 1993, "That became such a cliché certainly through the '80s, of the modern sensitive man, and it was wrong in many ways. . . . In the reading about that and the thinking about that, and observing certainly people around me, and how they behave and how they pretended they really were, it became a bit of an act of men pretending to be more sensitive than they actually were, and sometimes women pretending to be more aggressive than they actually were."

By musing about the spirit in his psyche, the "sister to the boy inside of me," Peart keys into a crucial idea, one that has been talked about a lot more in recent memory as the modern world learns to embrace gender fluidity. Humanity has been slowly moving toward a nonbinary approach to what defines a person. It's perfectly okay to be simultaneously strong and sensitive. If your sex is male, don't deny your sensitive side, and if your sex is female, don't deny your strong side. Balance the two, because as Neil expresses during the bridge, they're counterparts, not opponents.

"That's what I thought was so interesting about the word ['counterparts']," Peart wrote in the *Counterparts* tour book. "Considered in this way, contraries are reflections of each other, opposite numbers, and not necessarily contradictions, enemies, The Other. Polarities are not to be resisted, but reconciled. Reaching for the alien shore.

"Dualities like gender or race are not opposite but true counterparts, the same and yet different, and not to be seen as some existential competition—we could do without that. Better yet: we could get along without that."

It's all about balance, synergy. While Peart's lyrics vividly and passionately explore that inner synergy in one's own self, the synergy between all three members of Rush sounds magical on "Animate." It's also interesting, and a little bit ironic, that by simplifying their approach to recording *Counterparts*, it freed them to explore more than they'd expected, not only on a musical and thematic level but on a human level as well.

Life was good for Rush in the early to mid-'90s. After touring in support of *Counterparts*, Alex Lifeson recorded a solo project called Victor featuring such friends as Les Claypool from Primus and I Mother Earth singer Edwin, releasing the self-titled album in early 1996. Meanwhile Peart, always eager to learn new things, decided to completely relearn his approach to drumming, taking extensive lessons with famed jazz drummer Freddie Gruber and even playing on a couple tribute albums honoring the great Buddy Rich.

The guys would get back together in late 1995 to write and record what would become *Test for Echo*. Reuniting with Collins as producer, they strove to sustain the positive momentum of *Counterparts*, but as enjoyable an experience as it was for them, too much of *Test for Echo* fell flat. Aside from the ferocious "Driven" and the tender "Resist," the album is awash in meandering riffs, forgettable melodies, and some of Peart's weakest lyrics. The less said about "Dog Years" and "Virtuality," the better. To their credit, the album did well, making the top five in the US and Canada. The sixty-eight-date tour, billed as "An Evening with Rush"—the first time Rush had ever performed without an opening act—was a resounding success. On February 26, 1997, Rush were presented with Canada's highest civilian honor, the Order of Canada, and then a few months later received Canada's Governor General's Performing Arts Award for Lifetime Artistic Achievement. Early 1997 was a veritable love-in between Rush and their home country.

Things were going great. The album and tour was such a positive experience for all parties involved that after the tour ended in early July, Rush planned to take a quick break before writing another record. Mere weeks later, however, it would all change in the blink of an eye, and the future of the band would be put on indefinite hold.

Chapter Nine Playlist:

"Lithium," Nirvana

"Jerry Was a Race Car Driver," Primus

"Stick It Out," Rush

"Leave That Thing Alone," Rush

"Nobody's Hero," Rush

"Soon," My Bloody Valentine

"Nothing Natural," Lush

"Animate," Rush

"Dancing Men," Neil Peart

"Promise," Alex Lifeson

"Driven," Rush

10

"ONE LITTLE VICTORY"

Ghost Rider

On August 10, 1997, Selena Taylor, Neil Peart's only daughter at the time, died in a single-vehicle accident on the busy highway 401 between Montreal and Toronto. On her way to start university in Toronto, she was nineteen years old.

Inconsolable in the months that followed, Neil's longtime partner Jackie Taylor was then diagnosed with terminal cancer in January 1998. "After months of misery, despair, and anger," Peart would eventually write, "she never uttered a harsh word after that diagnosis, and rarely ever cried. To her, the illness was a terrible kind of justice. To me, however, it was simply terrible. And unbearable." Jackie succumbed to cancer on June 20, 1998.

Such an annus horribilis will break any person. "I didn't really have a reason to carry on," Peart mused. "I had no interest in life, work, or the world beyond, but unlike Jackie, who had surely willed her death, I seemed to be armored with some kind of survival instinct."

Out of respect for their buddy, Geddy Lee and Alex Lifeson sup-
ported Neil's decision to step away from the band to collect himself
on an extended motorcycle trip, with no set schedule to return. It
wasn't easy for Geddy and Alex to have to wait for postcard updates
just to find out if Neil was okay, but space was what he needed. His
solo journey, ridden on his trusty BMW 1100 GS, would take him
from Quebec all the way west to British Columbia, then north to
Alaska, down through the American South, to Mexico and Belize,
and then back north to Quebec, to the tune of fifty-five thousand
miles in fourteen months. Peart would document his physical and
spiritual quest in the remarkable memoir, *Ghost Rider: Travels on the
Healing Road*, which would be published in 2002.

In the meantime, Rush was a business as well as a band,
employing many, and with the future so uncertain—constant
questions from the media about the status of Rush were
always greeted with a patient, reserved "We'll wait and see"
from Geddy—people had to keep busy somehow. November
22, 1998, saw the release of *Different Stages*, a mammoth,
203-minute collection of live performances from three different
tours: the *Test for Echo* tour in 1997, 1994's *Counterparts* tour,
and as an added bonus, a scorching 1978 set recorded at the
Hammersmith Odeon in London. The collection would be a
real treat for longtime Rush fans, and an especially important
document as *Different Stages* would be the only live Rush
album to feature "2112" performed in its entirety, recorded in
Mansfield, Massachusetts, in June 1997.

Geddy Lee took advantage of Rush's dormancy by making his own new music, collaborating with longtime friend Ben Mink (Mink had previously played electric violin on *Signals* highlight "Losing It"). Those sessions would result in Lee's debut solo album, *My Favourite Headache*. For Rush fans, this was the closest they'd come to new Rush music for the foreseeable future, and to Lee's credit, *My Favourite Headache* is a strong record that holds up well against the handful of good moments from *Test for Echo*. Most notable is the terrific title track, a nimble bass workout unabashedly inspired by close Rush pals Primus that morphs into a surreal tightrope walk between '90s alt-rock, progressive rock, and the heavy power of late-'90s Rush. Another strong moment, "Grace to Grace" would also find its way to mainstream rock radio in 2000, which, coupled with some positive press, would shine some much-needed light on a dark period for Lee and the Rush camp.

While Geddy was immersing himself in his own work, Alex Lifeson was admittedly lost for a while. "I don't think I played guitar for something like six months," he told Martin Popoff. "I like taking a break when I'm off the road, but it was nothing like that. There was just no love in it, and there was no love in a lot of things. It was so painful. . . . I started working with some other bands, doing some production stuff, a couple of TV projects, and Geddy did his solo record. It looked like the band was done."

By late 1999, the fog started to clear for Neil, and a new sense of purpose started to form. While visiting friends in Los Angeles, he was introduced to photographer Carrie Nuttall, and as he would write in *Ghost Rider*, a month later they were "deeply in love." He moved to Santa Monica in January 2000 to build a new life for himself, taking up yoga, smoking and drinking less, learning to love again while enjoying a newfound sense of stability. He and Carrie would marry in June 2000, with Geddy and Alex present among family and friends.

It was manager Ray Danniels who first heard overtures from Peart, not long after the wedding, that he might be willing to start making music with Rush again. He knew Carrie was curious about seeing Neil play drums, the one side of him she didn't know as much about. Besides, when you marry someone who is revered worldwide for having a specific, inimitable skill, wouldn't you want to see (a) your partner applying that skill firsthand, and (b) witness the adulation so many people feel for them?

Danniels knew how sensitive a topic returning to the band was to Neil, so he didn't push it. And the time did come, in late 2000, when Neil contacted Ray and shyly suggested he come to Toronto and have dinner with Ray, Geddy, and Alex. He hadn't played the drums in four years, and was justifiably cautious, and perhaps a little afraid. "He hadn't played in a long time, and he didn't know if his heart could go into the music as it once did," Lifeson would say a couple years later. "He had lost too much. From the very beginning, from that meeting, it was a very fragile, tentative thing."

It was decided that Rush would rent a studio for a full year, and with no set deadline, sharpen their chops individually, try to recapture their chemistry as a trio, and possibly work their way toward writing new music. Their work schedule would be three weeks at Reaction Studio in Toronto, one week off, with only a single technical assistant present during sessions. *Jam! Music*, an online division of the *Toronto Sun*, would break the news in mid-January 2001. Geddy told them, "We're trying to make this session as casual and relaxed as possible, considering all that has gone down in the last number of years, I think that is extremely important for us, to keep things emotionally humane. This project is about so much more than us making a record; it is about us coming back together. It is about the psychological health and welfare of all the people who have gone through a very difficult time. . . . I want it to happen, and I want it to happen in a very positive and natural way."

It was an arduous experiment, to say the least, but things started to slowly fuse. By their self-imposed June break they had written thirteen songs, and it was decided they'd bring in Paul Northfield, who had engineered the band's albums dating back to the early '80s, to coproduce the album, the recording of which would commence in August. It wouldn't be until March 14, 2002, that an announcement would be made: the new album was called *Vapor Trails*, it was coming out on May 14, and its lead single "One Little Victory" would be released on March 29.

With expectations from fans sky-high, it was imperative that Rush's first single in six years make a statement, and the euphoric "One Little Victory" was the perfect choice. And what better way to kick off such an important track than by putting Neil Peart front and center? After all that time off, and all the subsequent time spent building up his strength and stamina as a drummer, Peart attacks his drums with his trademark power, as though he never went away. His intro on "One Little Victory" is the Professor in full Keith Moon mode: his double-kick drums and snare all hitting sixteenth notes, hi-hat hitting quarter notes, with subtle accents placed on specific snare hits.

That Keith Moon homage was in fact intentional. "During the time I was rediscovering music, I was moving house and digging out old boxes of records, things I hadn't listened to in a long time," Peart told *Modern Drummer* in 2002. "I didn't want to hear more recent music, because it made me think about things. But the older stuff from my youth brought some measure of happiness. I went back and listened to some of the best of Keith Moon's playing. Re-examining how great Keith was at that time revitalized that part of my drumming. And yes, there were certain parts on this record where I thought, 'Let's do it the Keith Moon way.'"

Those ferocious opening bars sound chaotic at first, but listeners quickly hear a very clever pattern as Alex enters with an overdriven guitar riff that echoes the slick, distorted sounds of Linkin Park and Disturbed. Offset by a stop-start moment featuring chiming arpeggiated notes by Lifeson, the threesome jams for a furious fifty-six seconds, very much evoking the feel of "Overture" from "2112." Rush was back, and they hadn't lost a step.

The pace of that intro section also wonderfully reflects Peart's lyrical theme for the song, which is simple but so effective: to keep pushing forward through all the bad things life throws at you. After the song settles into the swaggering groove of the verses, Peart, through Geddy Lee, gets to the crux of it all. Lee pulls off a fun vocal trick to help drive home the insistence of Neil's lyrics, shifting to a powerful upper-register voice in the second half of the verse. It's some of Geddy's strongest vocal work in years, as Peart talks about surrendering only to things we cannot control. It's as though he's continuing to expand on the themes he explored on "Time Stand Still" and "Animate," but this time it's coming from a place of pain, grief, and intense self-reflection.

As Peart learned, it's very easy to let yourself feel defeated in the wake of tragedy, but remembering to embrace the little positives in life can go a long way toward healing. You had a really good cup of coffee; that's a win. You took some time to listen to music that makes you feel good; that's a win. You went for a walk; that's a win. You got some rewarding work done at your job; that's a win. Embrace it, Neil says. All those little victories soon add up.

As Peart writes in the second verse, learning to do so is often more difficult than expected. A person has to be righteous, strong, and determined in order to do battle with trauma, to be courageous enough to step outside their comfort zone, and to embrace change, embrace the fluidity of life. That's exactly what Neil had to do when he set off on his fourteen-month motorcycle journey, and although it took a while, he was able to return to his friends in Rush renewed, more vulnerable, embraced by his buds, healed.

Geddy Lee said on an episode of syndicated radio program *Rockline* in 2002, "There was something about that song that seemed just so darned appropriate for opening the record, and also being the first release for us in such a long time."

The rest of *Vapor Trails* holds up very, very well. "Ceiling Unlimited," "Ghost Rider," "Secret Touch," "Earthshine," and "Freeze (Part IV of 'Fear')" are terrific examples of the range the trio bring to the record, which just so happens to be the first Rush album since *Caress of Steel* in 1974 to not feature any keyboards. If there's one big issue with *Vapor Trails*, however, is that it's one loud album. The overly compressed sound—which was a common practice in post-2000s hard rock—greatly diminishes the amount of dynamic range needed for a song to breathe, making for an absolute assault on the ears of listeners, especially on headphones.

The sound of *Vapor Trails* bothered Rush as the years went by. "We've never been pleased with the mix, and particularly the mastering on it," Lifeson told *Modern Guitars* in 2009. "We were never happy with that one; there are a lot of reasons for that. We're to blame for a lot of that, the way we recorded it was very impulsive. We didn't spend a lot of time on getting sounds, and we used a lot of the stuff that we did in the writing phase, rather than re-recording things. So, to maintain the pure energy of what those ideas were, we gave up a bit on the sonic end."

Released in September 2013, *Vapor Trails Remixed* righted that wrong in glorious fashion, not only improving the overall listening experience by creating a lot more sonic space between instrumental tracks, but actually improving the songs themselves. "One Little

Victory" benefits immensely from the overhaul, the remix and remaster breathing new life into an already great song.

The sixty-six-date *Vapor Trails* tour focused primarily on North America, save for a very special three-date engagement in Brazil, which was Rush's first time performing there. Recorded in front of forty-thousand rabid fans in Rio de Janeiro, the 2003 live album *Rush in Rio* is the finest of Rush's many live releases, the band reciprocating the joy of the fans tenfold. The magic was indeed back, and Rush would ride that wave of positivity for the next dozen years, hitting a new creative peak in the process.

Chapter Ten Playlist:

"Bravado" (*Different Stages*), Rush

"Driven" (*Different Stages*), Rush

"2112" (*Different Stages*), Rush

"My Favourite Headache," Geddy Lee

"Grace to Grace," Geddy Lee

"One Little Victory" (2002 mix), Rush

"Ceiling Unlimited," Rush

"Earthshine," Rush

"Ghost Rider," Rush

"One Little Victory" (2013 Remix), Rush

"Tom Sawyer" (*Rush in Rio*), Rush

11

"HEADLONG FLIGHT"

A Measure of a Life

"Blah, blah, blah."

On April 13, 2013, after being ignored (and/or disliked) for decades by music industry cognoscenti despite selling tens of millions of records, Rush were inducted into the Rock & Roll Hall of Fame, alongside Quincy Jones, Albert King, Donna Summer, Randy Newman, Heart, and Public Enemy. After eloquent acceptance speeches by his two bandmates, Alex Lifeson took to the microphone and facetiously uttered those three words. And then, in a spontaneous burst of performance art that left Geddy and Neil standing baffled behind him, Alex kept going, telling the story of Rush's journey while only saying the word "blah." Over, and over, and over. It took a minute for the audience to catch on, but once they did, they were in hysterics. It was a masterful display of mimed comedy, and a wicked roast of the old boys' club behind the Rock Hall. The clip went viral, Rush fans adored it, and in keeping with the band's irreverent sense of humor, Rush put out a commemorative T-shirt featuring the classic 1974 Rush logo with the complete transcription of Alex's speech within the letters. That's right, dozens upon dozens of "blahs."

With Neil back in the fold with a renewed sense of purpose, Rush embraced all the good vibes around them and made the most of it, staying busy enough to have a product and/or tour to promote every year while allowing themselves plenty of time to spend at home with their families. Commemorating their thirtieth anniversary in 2004, Rush released the *Feedback* EP, a selection of loosely recorded covers of the guys' favorite songs from the 1960s. While it doesn't exactly fall under the "essential" category, it's nevertheless a charming trip back in time. Geddy, Alex, and Neil sound loose, comfortable, and happy, especially on such highlights as "Summertime Blues" (modeled after both Blue Cheer and the Who), Buffalo Springfield's "Mr. Soul," Love's "Seven and Seven Is," and Cream's "Crossroads." Rush had not sounded this groovy since their first album, and it's a joy to hear this side of the band. It's not so much "Rush" as simply three buddies banging out covers in the garage on the weekend.

The band commenced writing their eighteenth album in January 2006, working together on and off before completing thirteen songs by fall. The process was a much happier and stress-free experience than the *Vapor Trails* ordeal, and under the guidance of producer Nick Raskulinecz—who had worked on terrific albums by Foo Fighters, Velvet Revolver, Killing Joke, and Goatsnake—*Snakes & Arrows* was completed in just five weeks. Released on

May 1, 2007, *Snakes & Arrows* was a huge step forward from *Vapor Trails*, the band's most nuanced material since *Counterparts*. The explosive "Far Cry" would become a rousing live staple, "Spindrift" is a clinic in musical tension and release, while "Armor and Sword" and "Workin' Them Angels" are wonderful showcases for Lifeson's range as a guitarist. And you know Rush is having fun when an album features no fewer than three instrumentals ("The Main Monkey Business," "Hope," and the *Team America*–quoting "Malignant Narcissism"), all of which are vibrant, adventurous, and laced with humor.

After touring for *Snakes & Arrows* in 2007 and 2008, the band collaborated with Canadian filmmakers Sam Dunn and Scot McFadyen on the feature-length documentary film *Rush: Beyond the Lighted Stage*. A love letter to All Things Rush, featuring scads of celebrity fans and candid, often hilarious interviews with Geddy, Alex, and Neil, it was an instant hit with fans. Better yet, it helped expand Rush's audience. What used to be a predominantly male fanbase in the '70s and '80s grew into something a lot more diverse after 2008, in large part to the charming friendship that was depicted in the film. Search YouTube today, and you'll see young people of all races and genders from all over the world jamming along to classic Rush songs. It's a beautiful thing.

As Rush celebrated the thirtieth anniversary of *Moving Pictures* with the Time Machine Tour in 2010 and 2011—the only time the band performed *Moving Pictures* in its entirety—plans for another new album were in the works, and it was an especially ambitious project for a band in its autumn years. The first and only concept album Rush ever recorded, *Clockwork Angels* is a steampunk bildungsroman setting, in which its young protagonist "travels across a lavish and colorful world of steampunk and alchemy, with lost cities, pirates, anarchists, exotic carnivals, and a rigid Watchmaker who imposes precision on every aspect of daily life."

While Geddy and Alex worked on the music, Neil threw himself into the storyline he'd imagined, writing and rewriting lyrics that further expanded on the idea. At the same time, Peart began collaborating with science fiction novelist Kevin J. Anderson on a novelization of *Clockwork Angels*, to be released at the same time as the album.

With so many moving parts, it took a while for *Clockwork Angels* to be completed. Rush teased fans in the summer of 2010 with two new songs: the dynamic "Caravan," which introduces the main character, and the thunderous power trio jam "BU2B," featuring the heaviest Rush riff in decades. However, it would be another two years before the finished album would hit stores and streaming platforms, which, after the tantalizing "Caravan/BU2B" teaser, made for an agonizing wait for fans.

Completed in the last few months of 2011 with Raskulinecsz again at the helm—who truly had a knack for bringing the best out of Rush—*Clockwork Angels* is a sort of miracle, a baroque masterpiece by a band who could easily have gotten away with resting on its laurels at this stage in their career. Musically, it's a rich album, as Lee and Lifeson showcase their extraordinary chemistry, creating an instrumental arc that mirrors Peart's story arc gracefully. The peaks and valleys of the protagonist's adventures are vividly depicted on such standouts as "Carnies," "Halo Effect," and "Seven Cities of Gold."

Then, in its final third, *Clockwork Angels* reaches a level of profundity and reflection that hints at something much deeper than just a fantasy story. Peart's lyrics are more introspective, as though he realizes he shares a lot more in common with his fictional story than he'd originally thought, and Lee and Lifeson sense this, the music complementing the increasingly poignant lyrics with emotional, affecting arrangements. "The Wreckers," built around a riff seemingly lifted from the Byrds, is shockingly beautiful, Lee's fifty-eight-year-old voice finding a new, more mature strength he hadn't shown before. All the while, Peart drives the storyline to a moving denouement while at the same time writing about himself. When that emotional resonance clicks with the listener during "The Wreckers," the effect is extraordinary.

It all comes to a head on the incendiary, transcendent "Headlong Flight," in which Peart and the protagonist become one, the band sounding absolutely on fire as they churn out an intro section that contains more than a few nods to 1975's "Bastille Day." ("What was it that Oscar Wilde said: self-plagiarism is style?" Peart joked in 2012.) "'Headlong Flight' was one of those songs that was a joy to write and record from beginning to end," Lee told *Rolling Stone* in 2012. "Alex and I assembled the song to be an instrumental and its original title was 'Take That Lampshade Off Yo Head!,' but once we saw the lyrics Neil had written, I knew that the spirit of the lyrics matched the instrumental perfectly and it was just a matter of making them fit and writing the melodies."

"I think the music marries extremely well with the lyrics," Lifeson told *MusicRadar*. "There's so many parts that are extremely dynamic. Most of all, we got to play like crazy. We wanted a song where we could stretch out like we do live with 'Working Man.' We did shrink the middle section quite a bit. Originally, it had more of a jam thing going on, but we thought it was a little over the top, so we pulled it back. But there's certainly more than enough there."

Neil Peart added some key insight into "Headlong Flight," writing in 2012, "[Freddie Gruber] was reminiscing among friends and former students. Often he would shake his head and say, 'I had quite a ride. I wish I could do it all again.' That is not a feeling I have ever shared about the past. I remain glad that I don't have to do it all again. While working on the lyrics for 'Headlong Flight,' the last song written for *Clockwork Angels*, I tried to summarize my character's life and adventures. My own ambivalence colored the verses, while Freddie's words inspired the chorus 'I wish that I could live it all again.'"

As the song launches into a hard-driving, four-on-the-floor tempo, Peart, via Lee, opens up like he hadn't before, proud of how he handled all the adversity life had thrown at him, while at the same time remembering what his beloved drum teacher had said. If only to experience the euphoria of all those amazing first experiences just one more time.

Because the song is built from the remnants of a fairly progressive instrumental, its structure is unorthodox. Rather than the comfortable formula of verse-chorus-verse-chorus-bridge-chorus, there's a verse, a first chorus, another verse, and then a completely different second chorus, played at half-speed. That downshift in tempo allows Neil to really hammer home his most poignant lines. The young man is looking back at all the adventures that brought him to the pivotal point in the story, and Neil Peart, the cyclist and biker who always stubbornly kept his gaze forward throughout his life, catches himself reminiscing about the four-decade ride he and his bandmates endured, exhibiting tremendous vulnerability, and the effect is powerful.

It's as though Neil feels, for a split second, the looming specter of mortality, but as he moves on to the next verse, he rights himself and focuses again on what's most important—the happy life he built for himself over the previous decade—and embraces it all, good and bad. *Il ne regrette rien.*

Alchemy, both physical and metaphysical, literal and abstract, is a recurring theme of *Clockwork Angels*, and the alchemy between Geddy, Alex, and Neil is delightful on "Headlong Flight," as the interaction between the trio feels telepathic. Lee's bassline is lively, forceful, and melodic, Lifeson has moments during the extended middle section where he shreds as though his life depends on it, and Peart is locked in, hitting the drums hard, punctuating passages with fills that only he could come up with. It seems fitting that the last song written for Rush's final album would so perfectly capture what made Rush so special.

No one knew *Clockwork Angels* would be Rush's final album, but that sense of finality was hard to ignore when the album came out. You couldn't help but wonder if Neil was saying goodbye on the closing track "The Garden" when he wrote, "The treasure of a life is a measure of love and respect / The way you live, the gifts that you give / In the fullness of time / Is the only return that you expect." Little did anyone know at the time that, in a way, he was.

After a highly successful 2012 and 2013—an instant classic of an album, a well-received tour, the Rock Hall induction—Lee and Lifeson started entertaining thoughts of a fortieth anniversary tour in 2015. Lifeson had been battling psoriatic arthritis but was in good enough condition to hit the road. Neil, however, was starting to feel the aftereffects of decades of hitting drums with so much force for four decades. Tendinitis and shoulder pain was becoming a big issue, but he still felt loyal to his two best friends and reluctantly agreed to tour North America.

The R40 tour would be a magical farewell, featuring an epic, career-spanning setlist that started at *Clockwork Angels* and went in reverse chronology, into the '90s, the '80s synth era, the prog rock god '70s, and ending with a rousing jam of "What You're Doing," "Working Man," and a few bars of that old, unreleased nugget "Garden Road." All the while the road crew would be dismantling the stage, gradually stripping it down until all that was left was a modest drum kit and a pair of amps propped on chairs. Geddy and

Alex loved every minute of it, playing a different guitar or bass for each song, and the tour was so fun for them that they were eager to expand it to Europe and perhaps beyond.

Neil, though, had a brutal time on the tour, battling severe pain throughout, requiring intense massage therapy just to get through each day. He knew deep down that this would be his final tour, and years later Lee and Lifeson would reflect at how disappointed they were when Peart told them he was done. After they took their final bow at the end of the Los Angeles show, with Neil stepping to the front of the stage for the first time in decades to commemorate the milestone, it became, if you will, A Tale of Two Dressing Rooms. Neil's dressing room was jubilant, as an impromptu retirement party with family and friends kicked into high gear. Meanwhile, Geddy and Alex politely mingled with guests in their room, quietly shattered that this wildly successful tour was over. Because they loved Neil so much, they respected his decision, but the inner heartache was real.

Months after the tour ended, Peart told *Drumhead* magazine, "Lately Olivia has been introducing me to new friends at school as 'My dad—he's a retired drummer.' True to say—funny to hear. And it does not pain me to realize that, like all athletes, there comes a time to . . . take yourself out of the game."

Lee and Lifeson, who were working on the R40 concert film and album, became a little bitter. Lee would later write in his excellent 2023 autobiography *My Effin' Life* that he felt some unresolved resentment toward Neil, and that there was some tension between the three going into 2016.

Over the next few years, the Rush machine carried on, reissuing *2112*, *A Farewell to Kings*, and *Hemispheres* in expanded deluxe editions that pleased fans immensely. Then, on January 10, 2020, Neil Peart's family made the shocking announcement that he had died from glioblastoma, an aggressive form of brain cancer, on January 7. He had been diagnosed in the summer of 2016, and as per his wishes, his illness was kept a closely guarded secret while he quietly spent his remaining days with his young family.

As the band, management, and Peart's family expected, the music world was blindsided by the news. As the flurry of tributes kicked into high gear over the following days, there was still a sense of disbelief that such a secret could be held so tightly for that long. Lee would talk about how difficult those three years were. Not only did he have to keep such terrible news to himself for all that time— all the while constantly being asked how Neil was doing and if Rush would ever return—but he had also to watch his close friend die from a horrible, horrible disease. But give Geddy, Alex, Ray Danniels, and the entire Rush camp credit: they followed Neil's wishes to a tee, which showed just how much mutual respect there was between everyone.

While it was sad to see the band all but call it quits in 2015, Neil's death was a brutal statement of finality, and in the years since, fans have had to come to terms with that stark reality. But that's where melancholy gives way to joy, because what a magnificent gift the boys have given the world: nineteen studio albums (each one significantly different than the next), eleven live albums, countless compilations, concert films, music videos. Rush's body of work is a rich, miraculous thing, always there to bring joy, catharsis, and insight to our lives. Rush's was a life very well lived, a tale of three friends who never left one another until illness cruelly took one of them away.

It was all done on their own terms, without a whit of compromise, delivered with charm, imagination, innovation, constant reinvention, magnanimity, humility, humor, friendship, and love. Rush's music is truly the measure of a life well lived.

A measure of a band.

And blah, blah, blah.

Chapter Eleven Playlist:

"Summertime Blues," Rush

"Crossroads," Rush

"Far Cry," Rush

"Armor & Sword," Rush

"The Main Monkey Business," Rush

"Vital Signs" (*Time Machine: Live in Cleveland*), Rush